Laptops
Just the Steps™
FOR
DUMMIES®

by Ryan Williams

WILEY

Wiley Publishing, Inc.

Laptops Just the Steps™ For Dummies®

Published by
Wiley Publishing, Inc.
111 River Street
Hoboken, NJ 07030-5774
www.wiley.com

WILEY

About the Author

Ryan Williams is the author of *Windows XP Digital Music For Dummies* and *Teach Yourself VISUALLY Bass Guitar*. He is also a co-author of *MySpace For Dummies* and *Expert Podcasting Practices For Dummies* (all from Wiley Publishing). He speaks frequently on technical and musical topics at a variety of conferences. Finally, Ryan has seen and repaired just about everything that can go wrong with a computer.

Dedication

This book is for Jennifer, my wife, partner, and number-one support client.

Author's Acknowledgments

This work would not have been possible without the tireless efforts of Greg Croy, Nicole Sholly, Rebecca Whitney, Lee Musick, and the rest of the Wiley team. A great amount of thanks is also due to the technicians and IT professionals who shared their knowledge with me. Nobody learns everything on their own.

Publisher's Acknowledgments

We're proud of this book; please send us your comments through our online registration form located at www.dummies.com/register/.

Some of the people who helped bring this book to market include the following:

Acquisitions, Editorial

Project Editor: Nicole Sholly

Executive Editor: Greg Croy

Copy Editor: Rebecca Whitney

Technical Editor: Lee Musick

Editorial Manager: Kevin Kirschner

Editorial Assistant: Amanda Foxworth

Sr. Editorial Assistant: Cherie Case

Cartoons: Rich Tennant (www.the5thwave.com)

Composition Services

Project Coordinator: Katherine Key

Layout and Graphics: Melanee Habig, Joyce Haughey

Proofreaders: Melissa Bronnenberg, Jacqueline Brownstein, Caitie Kelly, Dwight Ramsey

Indexer: Sherry Massey

Publishing and Editorial for Technology Dummies

    Richard Swadley, Vice President and Executive Group Publisher

    Andy Cummings, Vice President and Publisher

    Mary Bednarek, Executive Acquisitions Director

    Mary C. Corder, Editorial Director

Publishing for Consumer Dummies

    Diane Graves Steele, Vice President and Publisher

Composition Services

    Gerry Fahey, Vice President of Production Services

    Debbie Stailey, Director of Composition Services

Contents at a Glance

*I*t has been awhile since computers were the size of city blocks and operated by people wearing pocket protectors and oversized glasses. When you buy a laptop, you're getting the power of modern computing in a small, sleek package. Your purchase may seem complicated at first, but that's why you bought this book, isn't it? After you read through the tasks in this book, your laptop will no longer seem like a complicated package. And, unlike a package that's the size of an entire city block, you can toss this one in a bag and take it to your next business meeting.

About This Book

Laptops Just The Steps For Dummies doesn't read like a novel or a traditional how-to book. Gathered on these pages are straight, simple tasks that take you where you want to go with a minimum of steps. Each task lays out a specific goal and gets you there with a series of steps, paired with informational tips and helpful graphics. All the tasks are gathered together in parts, but you can skip ahead to what you need to know right now. Take it all in or use it as a reference — this book will help you find out what you want, when you want it to happen.

Why You Need This Book

Even if you have experience with computers, a laptop is a different animal. Because it comes in a compact package, you have to know different tricks and shortcuts to working with laptops. After you review this book, you'll know the best ways to work with your laptop (and how to keep it working correctly). The book also makes a great reference because you can jump to exactly the topic you want to review. Simply put, this book gets you started and keeps you going.

Introduction

Conventions used in this book

➡ Working your way through a menu sometimes requires several steps. When you see the ⇨ symbol, it means you're choosing that selection on the way to your final destination.

➡ Any time you see a word in *italics*, I'm introducing a new term that you'll see later.

➡ When you see the Tip icon, you should take a look at some additional — and helpful — information, even if it isn't part of the steps.

How This Book Is Organized

Each task stands on its own, but they're grouped under the following parts for ease of use:

Part I: Knowing Your Laptop

Even if you're familiar with the basic components of computers, you should know where to find them on a laptop. Squeezing all those components into such a small space means that things are different now. Here, you find out how to deal with that difference.

Part II: Looking Over the Vista

This part ties together all of what you need to know about Vista's features. It's the operating system of choice for most laptop manufacturers, and here's where you find the basics. Even before you add programs, Vista handles most of everything you want to do. These tasks unlock the system for you.

Part III: Expanding Your Network

This part gathers together the facts you need to know when you connect your laptop to other computers and the Internet. Part III also makes sure that you connect in the safest, most secure way possible.

Part IV: Hitting the Road

From a hotel room on vacation to a boardroom or conference center, this part makes sure that you use your laptop in the best way possible.

Part V: What Could Go Wrong?

Like it or not, things happen. The difference between a crisis and a crisis averted is knowing what to do when it happens. This part collects the simple troubleshooting steps you need to know in order to keep everything running smoothly, from backing up your data to finding out why your screen isn't working properly.

Part VI: Options

The mobility and functionality of the laptop make it an ideal tool for doing business in your office or on the road, so the first chapter in this part shows you how to use your office tools at home or away. It also focuses on software included with Vista and Microsoft Office 2007. The second chapter gives you a quick tour of Windows Media Center.

Get Ready To

Are you ready to go now? Just go ahead and jump in. Pick a task and find what you need to know, or just start at the beginning. Whenever you read a "Get Ready To" section, you'll know that the tasks you want are just a page away. Get ready!

Part I
Knowing Your Laptop

The 5th Wave   By Rich Tennant

"He saw your laptop and wants to know if he can check his Hotmail."

What's in This Thing?

*1*f you're accustomed to using a desktop computer, it may take a little time to become comfortable using a laptop. Most of the same parts are on the laptop, but they are in different locations (and are usually a bit smaller). You also have to get used to a few different functions. This chapter takes a look at them and gets you ready to use your new machine.

Chapter 1

Get ready to . . .

Find Your Laptop's Connections

1. Look at Figure 1-1. Your laptop has a combination of these ports, although not all connections may be present.

   - You can use the USB and FireWire ports to connect the vast majority of peripheral devices.

   - Use the DVI or VGA monitor connections for external monitors.

   - Use the serial and peripheral connections for older printers, scanners, and similar devices.

      More recent laptops probably don't have these kinds of connections.

   - Use a card slot to add specialized devices that require a direct connection to the laptop's internal circuitry.

   - Use the headphone/speaker and mic jack to add audio equipment to your laptop.

      Laptop manufacturers might include different goodies on your laptop, including slots for memory cards such as those found on cameras, video cameras, microphones, and other devices. Look at the documentation that came with your laptop to find other pieces of hardware that might be included on your computer.

2. Look at Figure 1-2. Use the Ethernet connection to connect your laptop to a wired network, and use the Modem connection to connect to a phone line.

    Some manufacturers include different connections on their laptops. Consult your laptop's manual to see whether your laptop has any proprietary connections for you to consider.

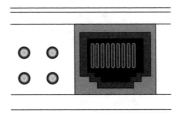
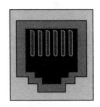

Ethernet   Modem

Figure 1-1: The most common device connections on a laptop

A   B   C

D   E   F   G

Figure 1-2: Your laptop's network connections

Use Your Laptop's Keyboard

1. Use the keyboard normally for basic tasks such as typing. This function works just like it does on the keyboard on any other computer. A typical laptop keyboard is shown in Figure 1-3.

2. Use the function keys (F1 through F12) to control the various hardware functions on your laptop.

3. Press the Fn key to access even more hardware functions.

 These hardware functions differ from laptop to laptop. Consult your laptop's manual for more specific functions.

4. Examine the keys for additional functions. For example, pressing the Num Lock key on some laptops makes certain letter keys act as though they're on a number keypad. These functions may change from computer to computer.

5. Press the Windows key (shown in Figure 1-4) to open the operating system's main Start menu, including programs and settings and more options.

Figure 1-3: The laptop keyboard

Figure 1-4: The Windows key

Connect the Power Supply

1. Plug your power supply into the wall.

2. Locate the power-adapter port on your laptop. The port is usually located on the rear or toward the back of the computer.

> The laptop has only one place to plug in, and you only have to ensure that the connection is tight.

3. Plug in the power supply (see Figure 1-5) to your computer. The laptop performs normally *and* charges the internal battery at the same time.

4. Leave the laptop plugged in until the battery is fully charged. It's better to let the battery run down completely and then charge it.

> Most laptop power supplies come in two parts: a power supply and the cord that plugs into the wall. For best results, make sure that both parts are connected tightly before plugging them in.

Use the Mouse and Pointer Stick

1. Look for the small, recessed pad near the front of the laptop. That's your mouse pad.

2. Drag a finger along the pad to move the cursor.

3. Use the buttons at the top or bottom (depending on the laptop) of the mouse pad to left- and right-click. See Figure 1-6.

4. If the laptop has a pointer stick, it's usually located in the middle of the keyboard. Move your finger to push the stick in the direction you want the cursor to move. Use the buttons as you would normally.

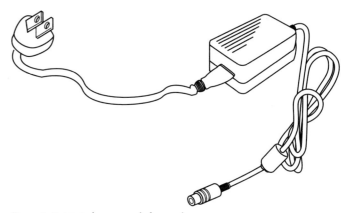

Figure 1-5: A typical power supply for your laptop

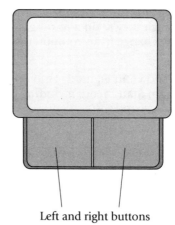

Left and right buttons

Figure 1-6: A mouse pad

Connect Speakers or Headphones to Your Laptop

1. Find the headphone jack on your laptop. It's usually on the side of the computer, as shown in Figure 1-7.

2. Make sure that any volume controls on the headphones or speakers are turned down all the way.

3. Connect the plug to the jack.

4. Slowly adjust the volume to a comfortable level.

 Some headphones, especially gaming headphones with microphones attached to them, may connect to the computer by way of a USB connection. You control these devices by using the software volume connections discussed in Chapter 8.

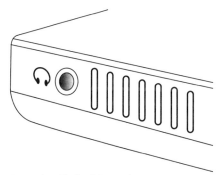

Figure 1-7: The headphone jack

Swap Out a Battery

1. Locate the battery for your laptop. It's usually on the bottom of your computer, under the palm rest. Figure 1-8 illustrates what a typical laptop battery looks like.

2. Release the switches (a laptop usually has two of them) holding the battery in place in the laptop.

3. Remove the battery and insert any other battery you want to use.

4. Make sure that the switches latch correctly. The battery is now ready for use.

 Some batteries have a switch on them to show how much power remains — without having to turn on the computer. Pressing that button causes a series of lights to turn on, illustrating how much charge remains in the battery. Otherwise, monitor the battery using the battery in the notification area.

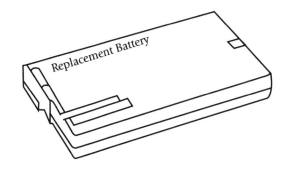

Replacement Battery

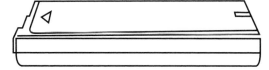

Figure 1-8: A typical laptop battery

Knowing the Right Switches

Chapter

2

*A*fter you're familiar with where everything is located on your laptop, it's time to turn the thing on! This chapter acquaints you with the best way to power your laptop on and off. It may sound simple, but you have to know a few tricks to keep everything working right. You also find out how to safely use Sleep and Hibernate modes to save time and power, and how to change these options to fit the way you work with your laptop. Finally, you find out how to save power by turning off your laptop's wireless devices and display.

Get ready to . . .

Power On Your Laptop

1. Make sure that your battery has an adequate charge or that the laptop is plugged into an outlet using the correct power adapter.

2. Locate the Power button on your laptop. The button is usually indicated by a symbol like the one shown in the lower-right corner of Figure 2-1.

3. Firmly press the Power button. Your laptop should start up automatically.

 This is the only time you use the Power button during your laptop's normal operation. Use the software commands to turn off the laptop.

 If your laptop fails to power up, check the battery and the power adapter again. It's easier than you might think for these components to become a little loose. If they both look fine, your laptop might have a larger problem. Check the manual provided by the laptop manufacturer to see which troubleshooting steps you should follow.

Turn Off Your Laptop

1. Make sure that any open documents are saved, and close all open programs by clicking the red X in the upper-right corner of any window.

2. Click the Windows icon in the lower-left corner of your screen.

3. Click the arrow button in the lower-right corner of the menu, next to the Power and Lock icons, shown in Figure 2-1.

Figure 2-1: The Windows menu

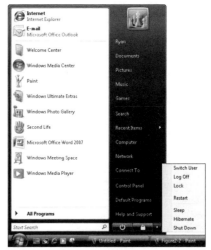

Figure 2-2: The Shut Down option

Use Your Laptop's Power-Saving Options

1. Refer to Figure 2-2 to see the other power options available.

   - Use the Switch User command to quickly open another user's account without having to close open programs or windows.

    You must have more than one user account on your laptop to be able to use the Switch User command. Read Chapter 5 for more information on setting up accounts for other users on your laptop.

   - Use the Log Off command to close all open programs and windows and close access to your account. Other users can log in to their accounts from here, but the computer remains on.

   - Use the Lock command to block access to your account while leaving the computer on. You must reenter your password to unlock the computer. You can also click the Lock button, shown in Figure 2-3.

   - Use the Restart command to shut down your computer and turn it back on automatically.

    The Restart command is most often used after you install new programs or updates or when your computer has to recover from a crashed program.

   - Use the Sleep command to put your laptop into low-power mode while you're away. Depending on your computer settings, you may have to use your password to log back in from Sleep mode. The computer is still on, though.

   - Use Hibernate mode to save all programs and windows to your hard drive and shut down your computer. When you power on the computer again, everything appears right where you left it. You can also click the Hibernate button, shown in Figure 2-4.

Click to block access to your account.

Figure 2-3: The Lock button

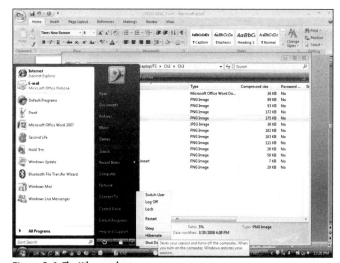

Figure 2-4: The Hibernate button

 Your hard drive must have enough free space in order to save this information. If you're running low on storage space, go ahead and shut down your computer instead.

 Your laptop may also have a Sleep button. You can just press it to put your computer to sleep. Refer to your laptop's manual to see whether this option is available to you.

Take Your Laptop Out of Sleep Mode

1. If your laptop lid is closed, open it.

2. Gently move the mouse, run your fingers over the mouse pad, or tap a keyboard key once or twice.

3. Your computer becomes active again.

 If you use an external mouse with your laptop, moving it may not wake your laptop because the power to that device has been cut off. Use the mouse pad or keyboard instead.

 You might need to reenter your password to access your laptop after putting it to sleep.

Take Your Laptop Out of Hibernate Mode

1. Open the laptop lid.

2. Press the Power button on your computer.

3. Rather than see your laptop start the normal booting process, you see a screen showing the phrase *Resuming Windows* and a scrolling progress bar. You then see the login screen illustrated in Figure 2-5.

4. You see your desktop, looking the same as you left it.

 You might have to reenter your password at this point to access your computer.

Figure 2-5: Resuming Windows

Turn Your Wireless Card On and Off

1. Either consult your laptop manual or look for a switch marked with an icon similar to the one shown in Figure 2-6.

2. Move the switch to the On position to activate the wireless card.

3. Your laptop recognizes the card and is ready to access a wireless network or join a network automatically, as shown in Figure 2-7.

4. When you're finished with the wireless network, move the switch to the Off position. The wireless card automatically shuts down and closes access to any networks.

   Deactivating the wireless card when it's not being used is a good way to reduce the amount of power your laptop uses. It can dramatically increase the average length of time that your battery lasts between charges.

5. If your laptop doesn't have a hard switch, you might be able to use a combination of keyboard keys to shut it down. For example, some models of laptops turn the wireless card on and off by pressing the function (FN) key and the F2 key at the same time. Examine your laptop manual to see whether a similar option is available to you.

   If your laptop has a Bluetooth card, you can use the same commands to turn this function on and off. Consult your laptop manual.

Figure 2-6: A typical wireless icon

Figure 2-7: A connected wireless network

Turn Off Your Monitor Automatically to Save Power

1. Click the Windows icon in the lower-left corner of the screen.

2. Select the Control Panel option.

3. Click the Hardware and Sound link and then select the Power Options icon, shown in Figure 2-8.

4. Select the Turn Off the Display option in the left column of the window.

5. Set the time frame in the two upper drop-down lists, shown in Figure 2-9.

6. To save power, the On Battery time frames are generally shorter than the Plugged In time frames.

Figure 2-8: Power options

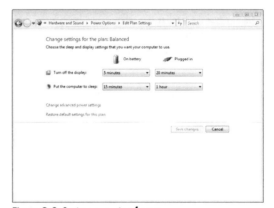

Figure 2-9: Setting power time frames

Tell Your Laptop What to Do When You Close Its Lid

1. From the System Settings menu, shown in Figure 2-10, select the When I Close the Lid option.

2. Use the drop-down menus lists in Figure 2-10 to specify the action you want to happen. You can also specify what the Power and Sleep buttons do.

3. Select whether you want your laptop to do nothing, sleep, hibernate, or shut down for each On Battery or Plugged In option.

4. Your laptop now responds the way you want in each of the listed situations.

Know When to Turn Off Your Laptop's Wireless or Bluetooth Connection

If you're not using a wireless or Bluetooth connection (symbolized by the icon shown in Figure 2-11), turning off that component can help save power and prolong your battery's charge:

➡ If you're using a wired network connection, turning off your wireless connection prevents possible conflicts among your laptop's network devices.

➡ Turning off your wireless or Bluetooth connection in public can help prevent your computer from being "seen" and potentially accessed by other computers or devices.

➡ When you're on an airplane, you aren't allowed to use devices such as a network or Bluetooth connection. Make sure to turn off your network connection before using your computer while flying.

Figure 2-10: Setting power options

Figure 2-11: The Bluetooth icon

Change Your Power Management Plan

1. On the Power Options menu, shown in Figure 2-12, notice the three default power management plans:

   - **Balanced:** This default option gives you a good combination of functionality while saving a decent amount of power.

   - **Power Saver:** If you'll be away from a charger for a long time (such as on a long plane ride), select the Power Saver radio button to prolong the battery life.

   - **High Performance:** If you'll be in the same place for a long time and can connect to a power outlet, select the High Performance option to get the most from your laptop.

2. To change the time frames for a plan, click the Change Plan Settings option under each plan's name and adjust the drop-down lists (see Figure 2-13).

3. You can change individual settings for certain devices for each plan by clicking the Change Advanced Power Settings link. To restore the default settings, click the Restore Default Settings for This Plan link.

4. Choose Shut Down, (as shown in Figure 2-2). Wait until the laptop completes the shutdown routine, your hard drive's light is off, and the screen is black before closing the laptop's lid.

 Closing the laptop lid before the shutdown process is complete puts the laptop into Sleep mode, which means that it's *still on!* Putting your laptop into a bag or case while it's in Sleep mode can cause overheating and damage.

Figure 2-12: The three default power management plans

 Change the setting back to Balanced when you're done with either of the other options. It saves laptop power (and your frustration level) down the road.

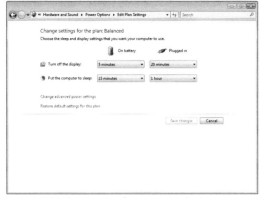

Figure 2-13: Changing times for your power plan

Going for a Drive

Your laptop is capable of using many types of disk drives for storage. Most information is stored on the *hard drive* (contained inside your computer), where the laptop gets all the information it needs to run Windows Vista and all the programs you installed. The hard drive also stores your documents, pictures, music, and other commonly used files. You can also attach *external drives*, like enclosed hard drives or smaller flash drives, to expand the amount of storage you can use. This chapter shows you where and how to store your most important data.

Chapter

3

Get ready to . . .

See How Much Free Space Remains on Your Drive

1. Click the Windows icon in the lower-left corner of the screen and choose the Computer option, on the right side of the menu, as shown in Figure 3-1.

2. The Computer window, shown in Figure 3-2, shows all drives connected to your computer and the amount of free space left on each hard drive.

3. For optimum performance, keep 15 to 20 percent of your hard drive free. As it becomes fuller, your computer slows down a bit.

Figure 3-1: Examining your computer

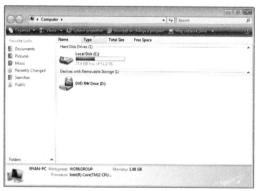

Figure 3-2: Your computer's drives

Clean Up Your Hard Drive

1. Right-click the hard drive you want to clean and choose Properties from the context menu.

2. Click the Disk Cleanup button in the Properties window, shown in Figure 3-3.

3. Choose to either clean up files only from your account or clear files from the entire computer.

4. After inspecting your system, Disk Cleanup displays a checklist of files that it can delete, as shown in Figure 3-4. You can also click View Files to see specific files you might want to remove.

5. Select the files you want to delete, and click OK. These files are deleted, freeing up your hard drive space.

 If you're unsure which files you need, wait until you know what you're deleting. Usually, files marked Temporary or files residing in the Recycle Bin can be deleted with no problem. Otherwise, do a little research first.

Figure 3-3: Hard drive properties

Figure 3-4: The Disk Cleanup checklist

Defragment Your Hard Drive

1. Right-click the hard drive you want to defragment and open the Properties dialog box shown in Figure 3-5.

2. Click the Tools tab and click the Defragment Now button, shown in Figure 3-5.

3. From the dialog box shown in Figure 3-6, you can either set up a regularly scheduled defragmentation or choose to defragment your disc immediately.

 Because you probably don't leave your laptop running all the time, the scheduled defragmentation probably won't work well. It's better to remember to defragment manually every week.

4. Let the process run. The computer notifies you when it's finished.

5. The defragmentation process moves chunks of data closer together on the hard drive, making file retrieval quicker and easier. Defragging your hard disk regularly keeps your system running smoothly.

 Depending on how long ago you defragmented your drive, it can take a little time. Let the process run completely before you move on to other tasks on your laptop.

Figure 3-5: Selecting the defragmentation options in the Properties dialog box

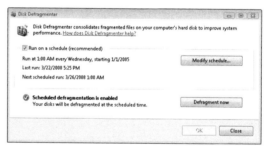

Figure 3-6: Choosing to defragment now or later

Explore the Contents of a Drive

1. Click the Windows icon in the lower-left corner of your screen.

2. Choose the Computer option in the right column of the menu. A list of drives appears, as shown in Figure 3-7.

3. Double-click the icon representing the drive you want to explore.

 In the case of an optical disc or external drive with an Autostart function, you can also right-click that drive's icon and choose Explore. You can then see the files and folders on that disc without opening any other menus or functions on the drive.

4. Double-click the folders or files you want to explore or examine.

 Be careful with the contents of the Windows and Programs folders. These folders contain files essential to the function of your laptop. If you're unfamiliar with their contents, just leave them.

 You can have more than one Explorer window open at a time. Doing so can be useful for comparing the contents of different folders or drives and assisting in transferring files back and forth.

Insert and Eject an Optical Disc

1. Determine whether your optical drive is a slot-loaded or tray-loaded drive:

   • **Slot-load:** Just gently push the disc into the slot. The drive grabs and inserts the disc automatically.

Figure 3-7: Choosing a drive to explore

- **Tray-loaded:** Look for the Eject button on the drive and press it. When the tray pops open, place the disc on the tray and push the tray gently back into the laptop.

2. Explore the disc as you would explore any other drive.

3. Press the Eject button to release and remove the disc from the drive.

 On a slot-loading drive, the Eject button may be located on the laptop keyboard rather than on the drive itself. Refer to your laptop manual for the exact location.

 When you're not using a CD or a DVD, keep it in a case or soft sleeve to avoid damaging it. If a disc gets scratched, it may become useless, and your data may be lost.

Shrink the Size of a Drive's Volume

1. Click the Windows icon in the lower-left corner of the screen.

2. Right-click the Computer option on the menu (see Figure 3-8).

 Make sure that your drives have different names so that you can easily tell one from another when you're exploring files.

3. Choose Manage from the context menu to open the Computer Management window, shown in Figure 3-9.

Figure 3-8: Options for exploring your computer

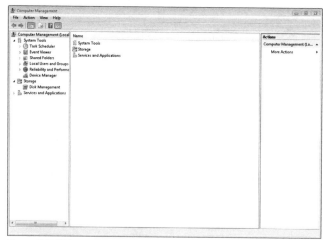

Figure 3-9: Disk management

4. Select Disk Management in the left column to view the active drives on your computer, as shown in Figure 3-10.

5. Right-click the drive you want to shrink and choose the Shrink Volume option from the context menu, shown in Figure 3-11.

6. The operating system lets you know how much storage space you can remove from your current drive. Select that amount and click OK. Your laptop now has a new partition.

 You can shrink volumes only on hard drives, not on optical media. After a CD-R or DVD-R is burned, that volume is permanent.

 Most laptops are supplied with only one partition on their hard drives. You might want to create a second partition if your laptop has multiple users and you want them to be able to access files outside their accounts. You can also create a second partition that will be encrypted for sensitive personal or business information.

Figure 3-10: Your computer's active drives

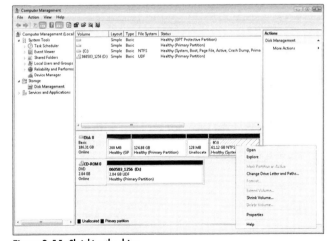

Figure 3-11: Shrinking the drive

Insert an External Hard Drive or Flash Drive

1. Connect the external hard drive to your laptop by using a USB or FireWire port.

2. If the drive has an external power source, turn on the drive.

3. After the laptop recognizes the external or flash drive, you see the window shown in Figure 3-12.

4. Choose the option you want to use. You can either open specific media files or explore the folders and files on the drive.

5. Now that the drive is connected, you can use it as you would use any other hard drive. To explore the drive further, click the Windows icon in the lower-left corner of the screen and select Computer.

Eject an External Drive or a Flash Drive

1. In the lower-right corner of the screen, known as the *notification area*, look for an icon with a green check mark on it. It's the Safely Remove Hardware icon, shown in Figure 3-13.

Figure 3-12: The Options for a newly connected drive

 In most cases, a smaller flash memory drive plugs directly into the laptop. A larger hard drive uses a cable to connect to the laptop.

 A smaller flash drive is powered by the laptop's battery or power adapter (depending on which one you're using at the time), which causes your battery to discharge faster.

Figure 3-13: The Safely Remove Hardware icon

2. From the Safely Remove Hardware dialog box, shown in Figure 3-14, select the device you want to eject and click the Stop button.

3. Click OK in the next window that appears, and wait until you see the message shown in Figure 3-15.

 If you're using or exploring the drive, you can't eject it. Close all applications and windows involving the drive before ejecting it.

4. Click OK. When you receive confirmation that the drive can be safely removed, unplug it from your laptop.

5. If the drive uses external power, turn it off now.

 You must use this command every time you remove an external drive from your laptop. Failure to do so can cause file corruption and damage the drive, especially if it's powered by your laptop.

Figure 3-14: The Safely Remove Hardware dialog box

Figure 3-15: Removing an external drive

Format a New Drive

1. Connect the new drive to your computer (as described in Chapter 10).

2. Click the Windows icon in the lower-left corner of your screen and select Computer.

3. In the Computer window that appears, right-click the drive you want to format and choose Format from the context menu, shown in Figure 3-16.

4. Name the drive and select the file system you want to use, as shown in Figure 3-17.

   • Select either the FAT or FAT32 option for smaller flash drives or drives you'll use on both Mac and Windows systems.

 You can use FAT only on drives that are 2 gigabytes or smaller, and you can use FAT32 only on drives that are 32 gigabytes or smaller. Larger drives must use the NTFS file system.

   • Use NTFS for larger drives that will stay on Windows systems.

5. Click Start and format the drive.

 You must format a new drive to use it on a computer, but the formatting process totally erases the drive. Do not format a drive you haven't backed up yet.

Figure 3-16: Formatting a new drive

Figure 3-17: Selecting a file system

Cleaning Up Nicely

*I*t may seem like a small detail, but keeping your laptop clean is an important step in making sure that your computer continues to run effectively. Its portability makes it more prone to damage than a desktop model, and the fact that most laptop components are integrated directly with the computer (as opposed to a removable keyboard or mouse) means that you might pay more to repair a damaged laptop than for a new desktop. Finally, keeping your laptop free of dust and grime lets it get more air and run at a cooler temperature, ensuring that it runs better and longer. This chapter contains tips on cleaning and caring for your laptop.

Chapter

4

Get ready to . . .

Clean the Keyboard

1. If the laptop is on, turn it off. Do not use Sleep mode during this task.

2. Use a can of compressed air (available at all office supply stores; see Figure 4-1) to blow any debris or dust off the keyboard.

3. Moisten a lint-free cloth with a small amount of water (no dripping!) or spray the cloth with a little cleaning solution.

4. Wipe the cloth over the keyboard lightly.

5. Wipe away any excess moisture or solution.

 Do not apply any water or solution directly to the keyboard. You can not only damage the keyboard but also cause problems in the circuitry of the computer!

Clean the Laptop Case

1. Using a can of compressed air, blow away any excess dust or debris from the case. Concentrate the airflow around any vents on the laptop.

 Do not shake the compressed air can before using. Shaking it can send moisture out from the can and damage your laptop components.

2. Spray some cleaning solution on a lint-free cloth or slightly moisten it (see Figure 4-2).

3. Wipe down the case.

4. Wipe away any excess moisture or solution.

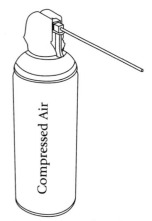

Figure 4-1: A typical can of compressed air

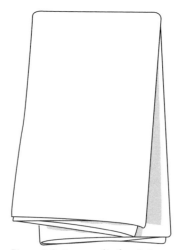

Figure 4-2: A common lint-free cloth

Clean the Laptop Screen

1. Turn off your laptop. Use a can of compressed air to blow away any dust or debris from the screen.

2. Put a little water or cleaning solution on a lint-free cloth.

 Make sure that the cleaning solution you use is approved for LCD or LED screens. Using the wrong solution can damage the screen.

3. Lightly wipe down the screen.

 You must use a lint-free cloth to clean your screen. Anything else might be too abrasive and scratch the screen. Also, do not use too much pressure because doing so can also damage the components of the screen.

4. Wipe away any excess moisture or solution.

Choose the Right Protection for Your Laptop

Decide whether a case, sleeve, or shell is right for your laptop.

➠ **Case:** Use a case if you will carry items other than the laptop or travel with it. When buying a case, make sure that it has a separate sleeve with at least a half-inch of padding to absorb any sudden shocks or bumps.

➠ **Sleeve:** Use a sleeve (see Figure 4-3) if you will transport only the laptop between different locations. When buying a sleeve, make sure that it includes at least a half-inch of the padding that fits completely around your laptop.

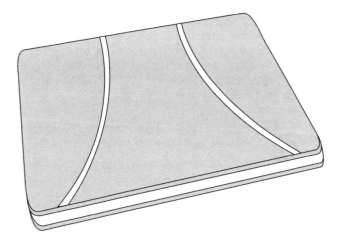

Figure 4-3: A laptop sleeve

➠ **Shell:** Use a shell (see Figure 4-4) if you're leaving the laptop in one general location and are concerned only with preserving the laptop case. When buying a shell, make sure that it surrounds your laptop but still allows for proper venting. Your computer needs to expel hot air in order to cool itself and run efficiently.

 Never insert into a case or sleeve a laptop that's powered on or in Sleep mode. You can cause heat damage to your computer.

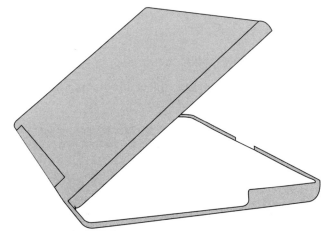

Figure 4-4: A laptop shell

Part II
Looking Over the Vista

The 5th Wave   By Rich Tennant

"Ironically, he went out there looking for a 'hot spot.'"

Accounting for Your Users

You may own only one computer, but that one machine can be of service to many different users. Even a laptop, which tends to reside with one user, may still have several different people who interact with it. To keep everything tidy and secure, Vista uses different accounts for each person. Each account has its own folders for storing data and retains its own preferences and settings.

This strategy goes far beyond just organizational matters, though. The type of account you use determines whether you can read or use certain documents, install hardware and software, and change certain aspects of the computer. For this reason, it's important to control who uses your computer and how much they're able to change things on it.

Chapter 5

Get ready to . . .

Create an Administrator Account

1. Click the Start button and select Control Panel.

2. Click the Add and Remove Users link under the User Accounts and Family Safety heading to display the Manage Accounts window, shown in Figure 5-1.

    The account created by default on your computer when you first set it up is an *administrator* account.

3. Click the Create a New Account link, type the account's new name, and select the Administrator radio button.

4. Click the Create Account button. You see the new account listed, as shown in Figure 5-2.

5. Use the new administrator account to install new software or hardware and make other significant changes to your system.

    You should restrict access to administrative functions to only the users who truly need them. A user who makes a lot of changes or installs or uninstalls a great deal of software needs to have an administrative account. If he doesn't, you probably shouldn't give him that level of control.

    Some software requires a user to be the administrator on her computer in order to be able to use it. Check the software instructions to see whether this is the case.

Figure 5-1: Adding and removing users

Figure 5-2: The new administrator account

Create an Account for Guests or Standard Users

1. Click the Start button and choose Control Panel⇨Add or Remove User Accounts⇨Create a New Account.

     If the User Account Control is turned on, you have to click to accept a warning message in order to complete this step.

2. Name your new standard user account and click the Standard User radio button, shown in Figure 5-3.

3. Click the Create Account button to complete the process. Your new account will be available at your login screen.

4. If you want only one user account on your laptop for others to use, just click the Guest Account icon, shown in Figure 5-2. You see the Turn On Guest Account screen, shown in Figure 5-4.

     The Guest account is accessible from the login screen without a password. Make sure that you want this level of access on your laptop before you activate it.

5. Click the Turn On button to activate the account.

     Have a standard account for day-to-day laptop use and an administrator account for special needs. Using a standard account ensures that nothing can be installed on your machine (viruses, worms, or spyware, for example) without your knowledge. You can log in to the administrator account to change, add, or delete programs and then log back in to the standard account to preserve the integrity of your laptop.

Figure 5-3: Creating the New Standard User account

Figure 5-4: Activating the Guest account

Alter Existing Accounts on Your Computer

1. Click the Start button and choose Control Panel⇨Add or Remove User Accounts.

2. Select the account you want to alter and examine the menu on the Change an Account screen, as shown in Figure 5-5.

3. Click the Change the Account Name link, enter the new name, and click Change Name to alter the account's name.

4. Click the Change Password link, enter the old password, and then enter the new password twice to change the account's password. This is necessary only if you've already created a password for the account.

 Make these changes only if you have the user's permission first. Doing so avoids complications down the line.

5. Click the Change the Picture link and choose a new photo to identify the account. You can choose a pre-loaded Vista photo or browse for images on your computer, as shown in Figure 5-6.

6. Click the Change the Account Type link to switch an account type between Standard and Administrator.

7. Click the Delete the Account link to remove an account from your laptop.

 Be sure to copy all information from a user account before deleting it. Removing an account means losing all information inside it.

Figure 5-5: Changing a user's account

Figure 5-6: Choosing your account image

Log In and Out of a User Account

1. If a laptop has more than one account on it, you see icons for each account. Click the icon for the account you want to access.

2. Enter the password for the account and click OK.

3. To log out of an account, click the Start button and then click the arrow button in the lower-right corner of the menu, as shown in Figure 5-7.

4. Select Log Off to exit your account.

    If you have any open programs or files, you may be prompted to close and save them before the account logs out. To avoid see this prompt, close all programs before you try to log out.

5. If more than one user will use your laptop in quick succession, choose Switch User from the menu shown in Figure 5-7.

    Choosing Switch User lets you leave programs and files open while another user is active.

6. Click the account you want to log in to and enter your password.

7. When you're done, you can log out or switch back to the original account, depending on your needs.

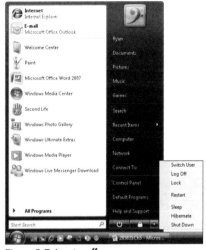

Figure 5-7: Logging off

 If you're done with an account for a bit, log out entirely to ensure that all your files are saved and secure.

 You have to reenter your password every time you exit or switch users.

Create a Strong and Secure Password

1. Click the Start button and choose Control Panel⇨Add or Remove User Accounts.

2. Select the account you want to change and select the Create A Password link.

3. Enter a new password in the text box that's displayed (see Figure 5-8). Strong passwords include

   • Capitalized characters

   • Numbers and symbols

   • Multiple words or chunks of text with spaces between them

   • Random but memorable strings of characters

4. In the Type a Password Hint field, enter a hint that will prompt you if you forget your password.

   Do not include your password in the hint field. That's the same as giving it away!

5. Click the Create Password button to enter your password. Notice how your choice has changed from Create a Password to Change the Password (see Figure 5-9).

6. Repeat Steps 1-5 to change your password.

   Don't forget your password. Having to change it later can cause problems when you want to access your account and its files.

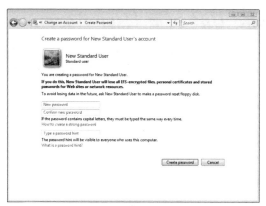

Figure 5-8: Creating a password

Figure 5-9: Changing a password

Set Up Windows Defender to Protect Your Computer

1. Click the Start button and select Control Panel.

2. Select the Check This Computer's Security Status link under Security to open the Windows Security Center, shown in Figure 5-10.

3. Click the Windows Defender link in the left column. If Windows Defender is turned off, you're asked to click a link to activate it.

4. Click the Check for Updates Now button to download all available data for the program to use (see Figure 5-11).

5. Click the Scan button at the top of the window to start the Windows Defender quick scan.

6. Click the arrow next to the Scan button to choose a full or custom link.

 Full and custom scans are valuable if you have rampant spyware infections or you suspect a specific Internet or network location has infected your laptop.

7. Choose Tools⇨Options in Windows Defender to examine the quarantine area for spyware caught in the scans.

 Windows Defender only protects against spyware and other low-level infections. You still need to use full virus-protection software, such as Symantec, Macafee, or AVG to keep your system fully protected.

Figure 5-10: The Windows Security Center

Figure 5-11: Windows Defender

Create a Local E-Mail Account on Your Computer

1. Click the Start button and choose All Programs⇨Windows Mail.

2. Enter the name you want displayed to the recipients of your message. (Usually, it's your full name.). Click Next.

3. Enter your e-mail address in the text box (see Figure 5-12), and click Next.

4. Enter your e-mail account's server information in the text boxes (see Figure 5-13), and click Next.

    Your e-mail address and server information are likely provided by your Internet service provider, your business IT department, or another, similar source. Check with them for more information.

5. Enter the e-mail username and password provided for your account and click Next.

6. Click Finish to complete the account setup and download any mail that's waiting for you.

    Make sure that Windows Defender is enabled and virus protection software is installed before you start using an e-mail account. This keeps infected messages from harming your machine.

Figure 5-12: Entering your e-mail address

Figure 5-13: Your server information

Create a Webmail Account

1. Choose a service for your e-mail account. Popular services include Gmail, Yahoo! Mail, and Hotmail. I use Gmail in this example.

2. Go to the Web site of the service you want and click the sign-up link, as shown in Figure 5-14.

3. Enter the information required for the e-mail account, including your full name, your username, your password, and any other security information, as shown in Figure 5-15. You're also asked to agree to it's the site's terms of service.

 Read over the terms of service before agreeing. You should always know what you're getting into, and you need to know how Google or another service might share your information.

4. After your account is set up, you can access your account by returning to the site and logging in.

 Webmail accounts may also grant access to programs such as Windows Mail or to mobile devices, depending on how they want their accounts to be used. Check with your service and shop around to make sure that you get what you want.

 Webmail is advantageous because you can access it from any computer at any time, just by going to the site. If you prefer a more private service or you already have an e-mail account, use Windows Mail or Outlook from the Microsoft Office 2007 suite.

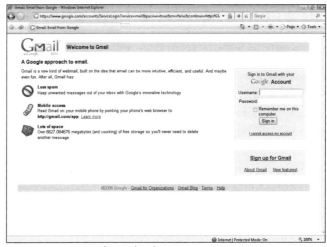

Figure 5-14: Signing up for a Webmail account

Figure 5-15: Entering your information

Set Your Computer's Time and Date

1. Right-click the clock in the lower-right corner of your computer screen and choose Adjust Date/Time, as shown in Figure 5-16.

2. Click the Change Date and Time button in the Date and Time dialog box, shown in Figure 5-17.

3. Use the clock and calendar to adjust your laptop to the correct date and time and then click OK.

4. Click the Change Time Zone button to adjust the computer to the correct time zone.

5. To automatically sync your laptop's time to an outside time source, click the Internet Time tab and enter the server address.

 The time is set to `http://time.windows.com` by default.

6. You can set up different clocks to monitor by clicking the Additional Clocks tab. Click the Show This Clock check box for as many as two additional clocks and set the time zones for each one.

 This strategy can be a handy way of monitoring the time for farflung relatives, friends, or business associates.

Figure 5-16: Adjusting the date and time

Figure 5-17: The Date and Time dialog box

Manage the Devices on Your Computer

1. Click the Start button and right-click the Computer link, shown in Figure 5-18. Choose Manage from the pop-up menu.

2. Click to select Device Manager in the left column of the Computer Management window that appears, as shown in Figure 5-19.

3. The Device Manager window shows a complete list of devices installed on your computer.

 A device that has a problem displays an exclamation point on its icon. Possible problems include incorrectly installed software and hardware malfunctions.

 If a device that you feel should be shown isn't listed in this window, make sure that the connection to your laptop is secure and the device is powered on.

4. To see the devices attached to each category, click the plus sign to expand the list.

5. Right-click a device's icon to update the driver software, uninstall a device, or check the device's properties.

Figure 5-18: The Manage option

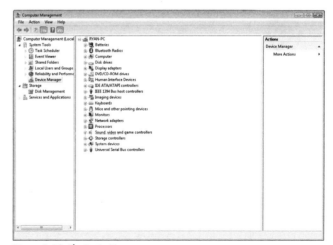

Figure 5-19: The Device Manager

Send a New E-Mail in Windows Mail

1. Click Start and choose All Programs⇨Windows Mail.

2. In the Windows Mail window, shown in Figure 5-20, click the Create New button to start a new e-mail.

3. In the Documents window, shown in Figure 5-21, enter the e-mail address, subject, and information.

4. Click the Spell Check icon on the menu bar to check the spelling and grammar in your e-mail message.

5. Click Send to finish your e-mail and send it on its way.

 Be specific on the Subject line. Not only will your recipient be able to determine at a glance the content of your message, but your message will also stand a better chance of making it past the spam filters.

 You can write an e-mail at any time, but it is sent only if the Windows Mail program is on while you're connected to a network. Until then, the message resides on your computer and waits to be sent.

 Click the Send/Receive button on the Windows Mail toolbar to force the program to send all items and check for new e-mail on your server.

Figure 5-20: Starting a new Windows Mail e-mail message

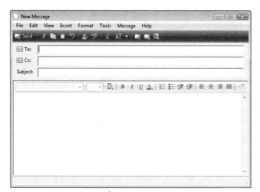

Figure 5-21: Entering information into a message

Attach a File to an E-Mail in Windows Mail

1. Click Start and choose All Programs➪Windows Mail.

2. Start a new e-mail message.

3. In the new message, either choose Insert➪File Attachment or click the paper clip icon to see the screen shown in Figure 5-22.

4. Find the file you want to attach, select it, and click Open.

5. The item is attached to your e-mail, as shown in Figure 5-23.

6. Finish the rest of your e-mail and click Send.

 You have to attach each file separately because you can't attach a folder. To send multiple files in one message, create a compressed folder containing the files you want to send and attach that file to the message.

 Be careful not to send files that are too large for your recipient's e-mail server to handle (under 2 MB, if possible). Your recipient's mailbox may not be able to handle large attachments that contain songs or movies, for example.

 Some e-mail attachments may be automatically filtered out of your messages by e-mail servers, which might view them as potential viruses. Always check with your recipients to make sure that they receive your attachments.

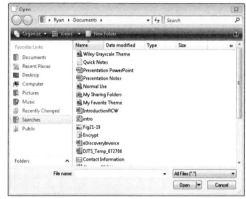

Figure 5-22: Inserting a file

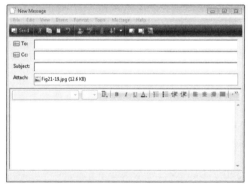

Figure 5-23: The attached file

Introducing Yourself to the System

*T*here's a reason that Windows Vista is known as an operating system: It provides the tools necessary for you to interact with your laptop and start the programs you need to use for school, work, or home. You can work with the operating system in a few ways, and this chapter introduces you to them.

Vista comes out of the box looking and behaving a certain way, but you can easily customize it. If you can change a feature and make it work more easily for you, you save time and effort. The tasks in this chapter show you how.

Chapter 6

Get ready to . . .

Customize the Taskbar

1. Right-click the taskbar and choose Properties to open the Taskbar and Start Menu Properties dialog box, shown in Figure 6-1.

2. If the Lock the Taskbar check box is selected, click it to free up the taskbar.

3. Move the cursor over the taskbar and notice how it changes into arrows, suggesting how you can modify the length and width of the sections in the taskbar (see Step 7).

4. Click and drag the edges of the taskbar to extend or compress it (see Figure 6-2).

5. To make the taskbar hide until you move the cursor to the bottom of the screen, select the Auto-Hide the Taskbar check box. You can also select check boxes to keep the taskbar on top of other windows and show the Quick Launch section.

6. To move the taskbar to the right, left, or top of the screen, unlock it and drag it to the side of the screen where you want to lock it.

7. Click the Toolbars tab to add or remove sections from the taskbar. Your choices vary depending on the programs installed on your computer.

 The Quick Launch section of the toolbar is to the immediate right of the Start button, and it's a good place to store shortcuts of commonly used programs and files.

Figure 6-1: Taskbar properties

Figure 6-2: Extending the taskbar

Change Your Start Menu View

1. Right-click the taskbar and choose Properties.

2. At the top of the window, select the Start Menu tab, shown in Figure 6-3.

3. Your first choice is Start menu, the default. Your other choice is Classic Start Menu, which is associated more with Windows XP and earlier Microsoft operating systems. If you want to work with Classic view, click the Classic Start menu radio button. Otherwise, you can leave this option alone.

4. To change individual details about either the Classic or default Start menu, click the Customize button next to the view you chose. The Customize Start Menu dialog box appears (see Figure 6-4).

    The details available for customization depend on which view you choose.

5. After you finish your customization, click OK to save your chosen options.

    You can easily undo any customization you choose by just backtracking and deselecting your choices. Don't be afraid to experiment and try different options.

Figure 6-3: Start menu options

Figure 6-4: Customizing the Start menu

Search Your Laptop's Contents

1. Click the Start button and locate the Start Search field at the bottom of the menu, as shown in Figure 6-5.

2. Type the name of the program or file you're looking for.

3. As you type, your available choices show up on the menu. The number of choices grows smaller as you continue typing.

4. Click on the choice you want to access to start the program or access the file, as shown in Figure 6-6.

5. To see more results than are shown on the menu (due to space restrictions), click the See All Results link.

 The Start Search tool can be a quick and handy way to find files hidden away in a long string of folders. A few quick keystrokes can save you a lot of time.

6. To expand your search to the world at large, click the Search the Internet link.

Figure 6-5: The Search window

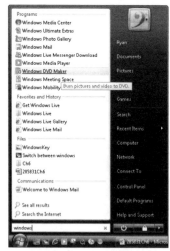

Figure 6-6: Selecting your results

Start and Close a Program

1. Click the Start button to open the Start menu.

2. The Start menu shows you a list of recently accessed programs, as shown in Figure 6-7. To choose one of them, click its icon.

 This option isn't available if you chose Classic view.

3. Click the All Programs link to see all software programs installed on your computer.

 In Classic view, click the Programs link to see the available software.

4. Click the icon of the program you want to open.

5. After you finish using the program, click the X in the upper-right corner to close the program (see Figure 6-8).

 Save your work before you close the program. Most programs prompt you to do so, but you should err on the side of caution.

 Close the program when you're done with it to free up resources and make your computer run faster.

Figure 6-7: Recently accessed programs

Figure 6-8: Closing a program

Switch Quickly between Programs

1. On the taskbar, locate the button for the program you want to work with (see Figure 6-9).

2. Click that item to switch instantly to that program's window.

 This is a helpful way to sort through multiple windows at the same time.

3. Alternatively, press Alt + Tab to open a window showing all active programs and windows (see Figure 6-10).

4. While holding the Alt key, continue to press the Tab key to scroll through your choices.

5. Release both keys to switch to a program immediately.

 Use this timesaving keyboard shortcut if you don't want to move your hands from the keyboard to the mouse.

Figure 6-9: Open programs have corresponding buttons on the taskbar.

Figure 6-10: Using the Alt+Tab key combination to switch between open windows.

Add Items to the Quick Launch Toolbar

1. Click the Start button and click the All Programs link.

2. Right-click the item you want to add to your Quick Launch toolbar.

3. Choose the Add to Quick Launch option from the pop-up menu, as shown in Figure 6-11.

4. Unlock the taskbar, if necessary.

5. Click and drag the edges of the toolbar to adjust the length and show all Quick Launch icons. You can also click the double chevrons (>>) at the end of the row of Quick Launch icons to show hidden icons, as shown in Figure 6-12.

6. Lock the taskbar again when you're finished.

 To keep the Quick Launch toolbar from becoming cluttered, restrict the icons on it to only the programs you use most often.

Figure 6-11: Adding an item to the Quick Launch toolbar

Figure 6-12: Hidden Icons in the Quick Launch toolbar

Use the Notification Area

Figure 6-13: The notification area

1. On the right end of the taskbar, shown in Figure 6-13, notice the notification area. It generally shows the icons of programs on your laptop that are running in the background.

Figure 6-14: Identifying a Notification Area icon

 A program that's *running in the background* is active and performing tasks, but it has no open windows and isn't under your direct control. You use the icons in the notification area to control different programs and processes, depending on your laptop's setup.

2. Hover the cursor over an icon to see the name of the process that's running, as shown in Figure 6-14.

3. Double-click the icon to display the options for that program or process.

4. Right-click an icon to see more options.

5. Depending on how many icons are in the notification area, you may see a chevron on the left end. Click that arrow to see additional icons.

 The notification area includes many icons related to system processes, such as audio or network connections. Use the shortcuts to avoid having to scroll through multiple choices or menus.

 Even if you can't see the programs represented in the notification area, they're using system resources. If you see too many programs in the notification area, open the program options and see whether you can keep them from starting automatically, if possible.

Activate the Windows Sidebar

1. Click the Start button and click the All Programs link.

2. Click the Accessories folder to expand it and view its contents.

3. Click the Windows Sidebar link (see Figure 6-15).

4. The Windows Sidebar, shown in Figure 6-16, appears on the right side of the screen by default.

5. Right-click the Sidebar and choose Properties to change its options, including which side of the screen it uses and whether it's displayed on top of all other windows.

6. You can add widgets to the Sidebar by right-clicking and choosing Add Widgets.

 Widgets are functions that appear in the Sidebar, including clocks and newsfeeds and other cool gizmos.

 The Sidebar uses system resources. If you don't use a widget, close it and, from the Properties menu you open in Step 5, set it not to open again.

 Some widgets require an active connection to the Internet to function.

Figure 6-15: Opening the Windows Sidebar

Figure 6-16: The Windows Sidebar

File It Away

From your weekly shopping list to songs from your favorite album to the huge presentation you're taking on the road next week, every bit of data you create or download onto your laptop is represented by a file. These items are stored on your hard drive and provide the content for the programs you use to create or do business.

Just like in real life, though, letting all these files lie around loose would cause confusion and disorganization. You'll notice that each user account on your laptop has its own, default set of folders available, and you can always create more. These folders help organize your information, and help both you and your programs find the information you're looking for. This chapter shows you how to move, create, and delete files and folders to keep them all useful and tidy.

Chapter 7

Get ready to . . .

Use Default Folders

1. Click the Start button and look for your name at the top of the right column of the Start menu.

2. Click your name to display the list of default folders, as shown in Figure 7-1. The following points can help you navigate this listing:

   • By default, files downloaded from the Internet are placed in the Downloads folder.

   • Documents are saved by default to the Documents folder.

 Creating additional folders inside the Documents folder helps you organize your files. For example, you can place text documents in a Text folder and store files related to your finances in a Taxes folder.

   • Your Internet bookmarks are stored in the Favorites folders.

   • Items and files on your desktop are shown in the Desktop folder, shown in Figure 7-2.

   • Folders such as Music, Pictures, and Videos are intended for media files.

 Although you can store any kind of files in any folder, most programs save files to the appropriate folder by default. You can change this behavior from inside the program, if you want.

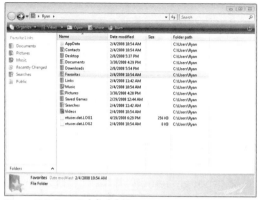

Figure 7-1: A user's default folders

Figure 7-2: The Desktop folder

Create New Files and Folders

1. Navigate to the location where you want to create the new file or folder.

2. Right-click in a blank area of the window to open the menu shown in Figure 7-3.

3. Choose New to list the choices shown in Figure 7-4.

4. Choose the item you want to create and click it.

 The types of items you can create from this menu depend on the programs installed on your laptop.

5. Type the name of the new item. The item you created is ready to be used.

 Make the name as descriptive as possible, but try not to make it too long. Shorter filenames are easier to manage.

6. Double-clicking the item automatically opens it.

Figure 7-3: Creating a new item

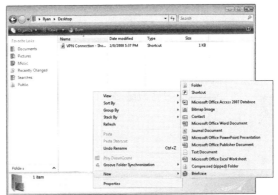

Figure 7-4: Choosing a new file or folder

Move or Copy Files and Folders

1. Navigate to the location of the original file or folder.

2. Right-click the item you want to move.

3. Choose Cut or Copy (see Figure 7-5).

Cut moves the file from one location to the next. Copy makes an identical version of the file and places it in a new location.

4. Navigate to the new location for the file or folder.

5. Right-click in the new location and chose Paste. The file appears in the new location, as shown in Figure 7-6.

With multiple windows open (the old and new locations), you can also click and hold the file you want to move from one folder to the next.

Dragging and dropping items can be unpredictable. Using the right-click menus is more precise and reliable.

Figure 7-5: Cutting and copying items

Figure 7-6: Pasting to a new location

Change the Name of Files or Folders

1. Navigate to the location of the file or folder you want to change.

2. Right-click the item and choose Rename from the pop-up menu, as shown in Figure 7-7.

3. Type the new name of the item, as shown in Figure 7-8.

     Avoid using special characters in the new filename. Characters such as slashes and percent signs can cause problems when transferring files from one system to another. Although Vista prevents you from using certain characters, stick with only letters and numbers.

4. Press Enter to complete the name change.

     You can't have two files with the same name in a folder. Change the location of one of the files before renaming it.

5. You can also change the name of the file by clicking the icon of a file or folder and then clicking the name (not the icon) and typing the new name.

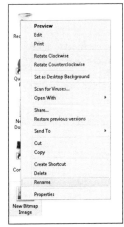

Figure 7-7: Renaming an item

Figure 7-8: Typing the new name

Delete Unwanted Files and Folders

1. Navigate to the location of the file or folder to be removed.

2. Right-click the item and choose Delete, as shown in Figure 7-9.

3. The Delete command moves the item to the Recycle Bin, located on your desktop.

 When the Recycle Bin is free of deleted files, it appears empty. When it has files in it, it appears full of crumpled paper.

4. Right-click the Recycle Bin icon and choose Empty Recycle Bin, as shown in Figure 7-10. The files are permanently removed from your computer.

 Files are placed in the Recycle Bin before they're removed permanently. Don't empty the bin until you're sure that you want to delete the files. After you empty the bin, its contents are gone forever. If you want to rescue a file from certain doom, just drag it from the Recycle Bin to its previous location.

Figure 7-9: Deleting a file

Figure 7-10: Emptying the Recycle Bin

Create Shortcuts for Commonly Used Items

1. Navigate to the location of the file or folder you want to access.

2. Right-click the icon and choose Create Shortcut, as shown in Figure 7-11.

3. A shortcut to the file or folder appears in the same location as the original item.

4. Cut or drag the shortcut to the new location, shown in Figure 7-12.

 Use shortcuts in central locations, like the desktop. Then you can directly access the file without having to navigate through several folders.

 Shortcuts help your data stay consistent because you can access a file from several locations without having to keep track of multiple copies.

5. Double-click the shortcut to open the file or folder.

Figure 7-11: Creating a shortcut

Figure 7-12: Moving a shortcut to a new location

Simultaneously Select Multiple Files and Folders

1. Navigate to the location of the files and folders you want to select. Choose any of the following ways to make a selection:

   - To select a few items from a larger group, hold down the Ctrl key and click the items you want to choose, as shown in Figure 7-13.

   - To select files and folders next to each other, hold down the Shift key and select the files and the beginning and end of the range of items you want.

   - To select multiple files using your mouse, click and hold the mouse in a window and then drag it over the items you want to choose (see Figure 7-14).

    If you use *marquee selecting*, the last method in the list, you can easily accidentally move or create copies of files. If you want to be precise, use the keyboard shortcuts.

2. You can now cut, copy, move, open a right-click menu, or open all the files as you would do with a single file.

    Performing this task can potentially open numerous windows on your laptop. Be sure that's what you want to do before opening files this way.

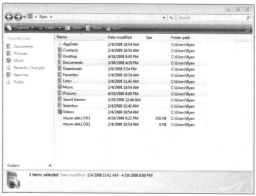

Figure 7-13: Selecting multiple items with the Ctrl key

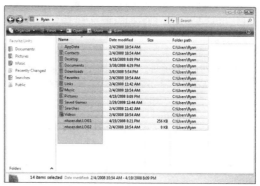

Figure 7-14: Selecting items with the mouse

Change How You View Files and Folders

1. At the top of the Explorer window, look for the Views icon, shown in Figure 7-15.

2. Click the arrow to see the available choices. You can select

   - Icons
   - List
   - Details
   - Tiles

3. Select the icon size you want to see, or move the slider, as shown in Figure 7-16.

4. Choose how to arrange the icons. Your choices are

   - **List:** Shows you just the names of the files and folders.
   - **Details:** Shows names and other information about your files and folders, such as file size and date-and-time stamps.
   - **Tiles:** Shows an organized display of your icons.

    You can set different views for different locations, depending on your needs.

    Click the View button to cycle though all four view choices.

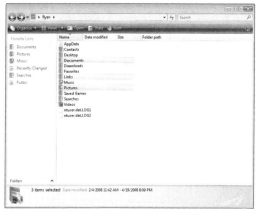

Figure 7-15: The View option

Figure 7-16: The Icon Size slider

Create Archives of Files and Folders

1. Select the files and folders you want to put into an archive.

    An archive compresses the size of the included files and folders and places them in one conglomerated file, which makes it easier to store and move multiple large items.

2. Right-click the selected items and choose Send To⇨ Compressed (zipped) Folder, as shown in Figure 7-17.

3. Type the name of the new compressed folder, as shown in Figure 7-18. The compressed folder appears in the same location as the original files and folders.

    Creating a compressed folder leaves the original files unchanged. To change the files inside the compressed folder, you have to open the archive and make changes from there.

4. To add files to an existing compressed folder, drag the file to the folder.

5. Double-click the compressed folder to open it and access its items.

6. To move all items from outside the archive, right-click the compressed folder and choose Extract All. The files appear in the same location as the compressed folder.

Figure 7-17: Sending files to a compressed folder

Figure 7-18: Naming a new archive

Resize Open Windows

You might find that your desktop has several open windows on it. The following points highlight how to navigate through them — whether you need to move one out of your way or look at something in a minimized window:

➡ **Minimize:** To minimize an open window, click the underscore in the upper-right corner, as shown in Figure 7-19. The window is removed from the desktop. Click the window's icon on the taskbar to display it again.

 If you have to have a number of windows open at the same time, this method is a good way to reduce clutter. If you don't have to have them open, however, it might be time to close some of the windows to save space and computer resources.

➡ **Maximize:** To *maximize* the window (make it fill the entire screen), click the middle button in the upper-right corner of the window. Click that button again, which has changed to Restore, to return the window to its original size.

➡ **Resize:** To change the size of a window, move the cursor to the edge or corner of a window until it changes to display a pair of arrows. Click and hold the edge or corner and move the mouse to resize the window (see Figure 7-20). Release the mouse when the window is the size you want.

➡ **Close:** Click the X in the upper-right corner of the window to close the window.

Minimize   Close

Maximize

Figure 7-19: Minimizing a window

Figure 7-20: Resizing a window manually

Setting Up Your Resources

*Y*ou're going to spend a lot of time looking at your laptop, so you might as well make it something you want to look at. Changing how your laptop's monitor appears can mean changing the size of fonts and icons for easier use or adding a picture of your family to the background. You can customize the appearance of Windows Vista in many ways to create your own, customized work environment.

Chapter

8

Get ready to . . .

Change the Size and Color of Windows Vista

1. Right-click anywhere on the desktop (except on any toolbars or icons) and choose Personalize from the pop-up menu.

    You can also click the Start button, select the Control Panel, select Appearance and Personalization, and then click Personalization.

2. Select the Windows Color and Appearance option to open the Appearance Settings dialog box, shown in Figure 8-1.

3. Scroll through the available color schemes in the drop-down list to see which scheme appeals to you.

    Don't worry if some of the themes shown in the figure aren't available on your computer. The use of certain Vista themes depends on your laptop's video card. If a theme doesn't show up, you can't use it anyway.

4. Click the Effects button to add subtle shadows or smoother fonts to your text and windows.

5. Click the Advanced button to change specific elements in each color scheme, as shown in Figure 8-2.

    If you ever want to reset the color scheme, just reselect the original scheme and click OK. All the screen elements return to the way they were originally, and you can start over or leave them alone.

Figure 8-1: Appearance settings

Figure 8-2: Changing specific color elements

Change the Screen Resolution

1. Right-click the desktop and choose Personalize.

2. Choose the Display Settings option to open the dialog box shown in Figure 8-3.

3. Adjust the slider to your preferred resolution and click OK. The Display Settings dialog box appears, as shown in Figure 8-4.

     The correct resolution for your monitor depends on many factors, including whether your screen is standard or wide-screen, how small you like your text and icons, and how powerful your video card is. Feel free to experiment.

4. Take a look at the finished product and select Yes or No, depending on what you want to do.

     Leave the Advanced settings and colors alone when working with your laptop. Unlike desktop computers, where you can use a variety of monitors in different configurations, your laptop has only one main monitor. Vista has already detected it and has set these options to their best available setting.

Figure 8-3: Moving the slider to choose the resolution.

Figure 8-4: Clicking Yes to confirm the resolution

Change the Desktop Wallpaper

1. Right-click the desktop and choose Personalize.

2. Choose the Desktop Background option to open the menu shown in Figure 8-5.

3. Use the Location drop-down list to select whether you want your wallpaper to consist of a solid color, a picture, or a video.

4. If you choose a solid color, just select it from the available options. Click the More link to see additional options.

5. For pictures or videos, select that option from the Location drop-down list.

 Windows Vista comes preloaded with sample pictures and videos, and you can also use your own images and movies.

6. Select a picture or video from the items shown in Figure 8-6, or click the Browse button to explore your laptop for a specific file.

7. Use the radio buttons at the bottom of the window to select how your wallpaper will appear. You can tile it, fill the screen with it, or position it in specific locations.

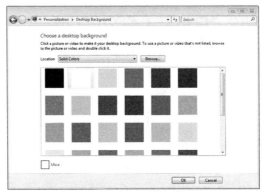

Figure 8-5: The Desktop Background dialog box

Figure 8-6: Choosing custom wallpaper

Change the Screen Saver

1. Right-click the desktop and choose Personalize.

2. Choose the Screen Saver option to open the Screen Saver Settings dialog box, shown in Figure 8-7.

3. Choose the screen saver you want to use from the drop-down list. The small preview window shows you what the screen will look like when the screen saver is activated.

4. If the screen saver has any variable settings, you can click the Settings button to change them, as shown in Figure 8-8. Not all screen savers have this option.

5. In the Screen Saver Settings dialog box, click the Preview button to show what the screen saver will do when it's activated. Move the mouse to end the preview.

6. In the Wait box, specify how long you want the computer to be idle before the screen saver kicks in.

7. If you want someone to have to enter a password to turn off the screen saver (a useful security feature), select the On Resume, Display Logon Screen check box (next to the Wait option).

 You aren't limited to using the screen savers that come with Vista. Others are available for download, either for free or a small fee. Be careful to download only from trusted sources, though.

Figure 8-7: The Screen Saver dialog box

Figure 8-8: Changing screen saver settings

Adjust the Sound and Volume on Your Laptop

1. Right-click the desktop and choose Personalize.

2. Select the Sounds option to open the Sound dialog box, shown in Figure 8-9.

3. To change the overall sound scheme, select an option from the drop-down list near the top of the dialog box.

4. To change a single element, select it in the scroll window and click Browse to select a .wav file to play when that event occurs, such as an error message or a new e-mail. Clicking Browse opens the browser window shown in Figure 8-10. Choose a sound and click OK.

5. To listen to the audio choice, click the Test button next to the Browse button.

 You can choose any .wav file from anywhere on your system, but make sure that it's not too long or too annoying. A file can easily sound cute at first and then become an extreme nuisance.

Figure 8-9: Personalizing sounds

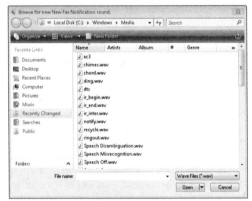

Figure 8-10: Browsing for new sounds

Give Your Laptop a Theme

1. Right-click the desktop and choose Personalize.

2. Select the Theme option to open the Theme Settings dialog box, shown in Figure 8-11.

3. From the drop-down list, select the theme you want to use. If you made several changes in the overall style and color scheme of your laptop, you can click Save to preserve your changes, as shown in Figure 8-12.

4. To use a theme you downloaded from the Internet, select Browse from the drop-down list (in the Theme Settings dialog box) and navigate to where you saved the theme.

 Make sure to download your theme from a trusted source. Using a theme means giving it access to your system settings, and an unknown theme can infect your computer with a malicious program or virus.

Figure 8-11: The Theme menu

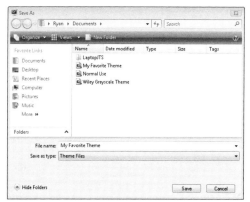

Figure 8-12: Saving the theme

Installing and Removing Software

*W*indows Vista comes with a great deal of functions included, but chances are that you will want some additional programs for your laptop. Whether it's Microsoft Office, iTunes, or another program, you have to add it to your computer. Although the process isn't entirely automatic, it is fairly simple.

This chapter describes how to put additional programs on your laptop as well as what to do when you want to free up space and remove those programs. Finally, the chapter tells you how to exercise control over how these programs behave. It's your laptop, after all.

Chapter

9

Get ready to . . .

Install New Programs

1. Obtain a copy of the program you want to install. Programs are distributed either over the Internet or by way of physical media, such as DVDs or flash drives.

Always use legally obtained software. Not only are you not breaking the law, but you can also access support and updates that make it easier to use the software. If you don't want to spend money, you can usually find free and legal alternatives on the Internet. A little footwork goes a long way.

2. Make sure that your hard drive has enough room for the program and that your laptop can run the program you want. The remaining amount of space is shown under the drive by clicking Start⇨Computer, and the software program lists the requirements that your laptop must meet to run the software

3. Insert the physical media or navigate to the location of the download and click the Install file (see Figure 9-1). This file is typically named Install or Setup, but the name varies from program to program.

4. Follow any installation instructions that are displayed, as shown by the example in Figure 9-2. Again, they vary from program to program.

Don't cancel or interrupt the installation. If you do, you can disrupt both the functioning of the program and your system at large.

5. Click OK or Finish to complete the installation. Depending on the program, you might be asked to reboot your computer.

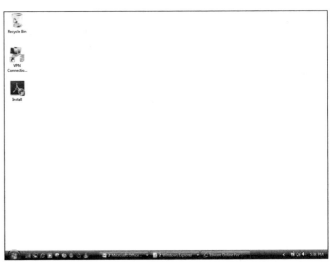

Figure 9-1: Double-clicking the Install file to start the installation

Pay close attention to the installation process. You're asked to choose where to place the program (usually, in C:\Program Files), where to place shortcuts and other icons, and whether you agree to the license terms of the software.

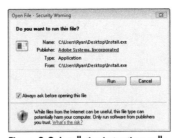

Figure 9-2: Installation instructions walk you through the process step-by-step

Uninstall Trial or Unwanted Programs

1. Click the Start button and select Control Panel.

2. Choose Uninstall Programs under the Programs header to open the Control Panel Home, shown in Figure 9-3.

3. Choose the program you want to remove and click it.

4. Verify that you want to uninstall the program, as shown in Figure 9-4.

    You can turn off this verification process by selecting the In the Future check box, but if you do, you can accidentally remove a program that you need, and you won't have the safety net.

5. Follow the instructions to remove the program.

    If you're having problems with a program running incorrectly, uninstalling and reinstalling it can sometimes correct the problem.

    This process also allows you to change the parts of the program installed on the laptop or to try to repair an incorrectly working program. Check your program's instructions before using these functions to see what you can accomplish by using them.

    Some programs included with Windows Vista, such as Notepad or Windows Media Player, can't be uninstalled.

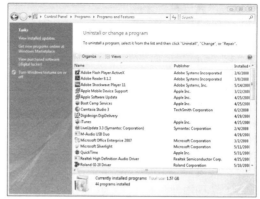

Figure 9-3: Choosing a program to uninstall

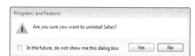

Figure 9-4: Are you sure you want to do this?

Set Program Defaults

1. Click the Start button and select Default Programs from the right side of the menu.

2. Click the Set Your Default Programs link to view the Set Default Programs dialog box, shown in Figure 9-5.

3. Click to select the program you want to use by default for a specific set of files. For example, if you want to use Windows Media Player rather than iTunes by default, click Windows Media Player.

4. Click the Set This Program As Default button, shown in Figure 9-6.

5. All associated files (such as music or movies, in this case) will now open in this program when opened.

 You can always go back and forth between default settings, if you want. Just repeat the steps to change them. You can make this change at any time, and for any reason.

6. To change which files a program can open, click the Choose Defaults for This Program link and choose files from the checklist.

 If you're unsure what the file types do, just leave them alone and change the default program instead.

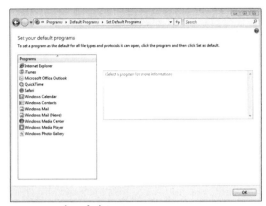

Figure 9-5: The Default Programs menu

Figure 9-6: Setting the default program

Change Which Programs or Files Launch at Startup

1. Click the Start button and select All Programs.

2. Right-click the Startup folder and choose Open to open the Startup window, shown in Figure 9-7.

3. Create a shortcut for the file, folder, or program you want to start and copy it into this folder (see Figure 9-8).

4. When you restart the computer, that item starts automatically.

 Keep the number of programs in this folder to a minimum. The more programs that start automatically, the more time it takes your laptop to start up. Having more programs also taxes more of your computer's processor power and memory.

 The programs in the Startup folder vary from user to user.

5. To stop a program from opening, delete its shortcut from the Startup folder.

Figure 9-7: The Startup folder

Figure 9-8: Adding a shortcut to the Startup folder

Force a Program to Open a Specific File Format

1. Click the Start button and select the Control Panel.

2. Click the Programs link.

3. Select the Make a File Type Always Open in a Specific Program link to see the Set Associations dialog box, shown in Figure 9-9.

4. Scroll through the list until you see the file type you're looking for.

 It's a long list, so be sure that you have the exact file type you're looking for before you make any changes.

5. Select the file type and click the Change Program button.

6. Choose the program you want to use from the list shown in Figure 9-10.

 Although you can use the Browse button in the dialog box to search for programs not shown in the list, you generally should stick with the selected choice. The program you want might not be the best choice to use.

7. Every time you click this file type, the program you selected opens.

8. You can change the program for individual files (not just file types) by right-clicking the file, choosing Properties, and clicking Change. You see a menu similar to the one shown in Figure 9-10.

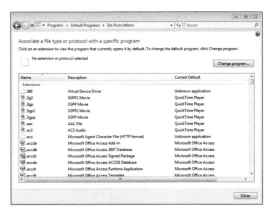

Figure 9-9: Setting file type associations

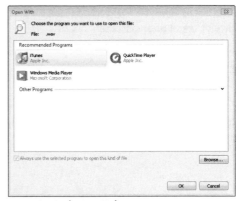

Figure 9-10: The Open With menu

Making Devices Play Nice Together

Chapter 10

A typical computer now has wired and wireless network connections, a Bluetooth adapter, an optical drive, an infrared port, and more. These items are in addition to the standard features on a computer (such as the monitor, mouse, and keyboard) that are already packed into a tiny package. Still, you probably need more.

Your laptop is capable of connecting to a multitude of devices that can expand your computer's storage and capabilities, and this chapter shows you the best way to connect those devices. You not only get to use some great toys, but you also keep your hardware and data safe in the process.

Get ready to . . .

Install Drivers and Software for New Devices

1. Insert any disc that the manufacturer gave you, or navigate to the manufacturer's Web site and download software.

2. Click the startup program to run it, either from the disc or from wherever you saved the downloaded file.

3. Follow the instructions to install the software, as shown in Figure 10-1.

4. Wait to connect or power up the device you're installing until the software asks for it, as shown in Figure 10-2.

5. You may have to restart your computer when you're prompted — you can't use the device properly until after you do.

 Discs with software may be helpful if you're not connected to a network during installation, but it's a good idea to check the manufacturer's Web site in any case. It may have updated software that can help your device run better with your laptop.

 Burn any downloaded installation files to CD after you're done with them. This Tip frees up space on your laptop and ensures that you have a copy available in case something goes wrong on your laptop.

 Most devices require administrative privileges to install new software and connections.

Figure 10-1: Installing hardware drivers

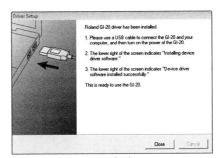

Figure 10-2: Connecting the device

Connect and Use a New Printer

1. Install the software and drivers for your new printer before connecting it to the computer.

2. For a local USB printer (a printer connected directly to your computer by a USB cable), connect the printer now and turn it on.

3. Click Start, select Control Panel, and click the Printer link under the Hardware and Sound heading.

4. In the Printers window, shown in Figure 10-3, right-click your new printer and choose Set As Default Printer.

   If you have only one printer to use, this step isn't necessary. If you use multiple printers, this step sets your printer as the one the computer uses automatically.

5. For printers that require a manual connection (such as a parallel port or wireless network connection), click the Add Printer icon.

6. Select your printer type from the list of choices (see Figure 14-4), click Next, and then follow the instructions for installation.

 Printers typically come with a great deal of software, such as ink-management programs and trial offers for other programs. If you don't want to use those programs, look for a basic install package that just puts the driver on your laptop.

 Most laptops don't have parallel ports any more, but the printers that use them connect on Port LPT1.

 Wireless, network, and Bluetooth printers should show up automatically when Vista searches for them. Sometimes, though, automatic processes don't happen automatically. Make sure that the printer you want to use is turned on and ready in case it doesn't show up the first time.

Figure 10-3: Setting the default printer

Figure 10-4: Connecting a printer manually

Use an External Keyboard or Mouse

1. If your mouse or keyboard comes with extra software, install it before connecting your new device.

2. Connect your device to your laptop.

3. For mice, click the Start button, choose Control Panel, and select the Mouse link under the Hardware and Sound header.

4. Set the options for your mouse in the Mouse Properties dialog box, shown in Figure 10-5. You can customize how fast the mouse moves your cursor, what to do if your mouse has a scroll wheel or additional buttons, and other options. This option applies to both the mouse pad on your laptop and external mice. Click OK after making your choices.

5. For keyboards, click the Start button and choose Control Panel⇨Hardware and Sound⇨Keyboard (see Figure 10-6). Click OK after making your choices.

Figure 10-5: The mouse control panel

Figure 10-6: The keyboard control panel

 Most external keyboards and mice have USB connections, although you may run into the occasional PS/2 connection on older models. Make sure that you're using the right connection before buying a device for your laptop.

 Some options on your mouse may require the additional software you installed at the beginning of this task. That's one reason why it's a good idea to install the software before you connect the new device.

 You may prefer the feel of an external mouse, or you may want to use additional features on an external keyboard, such as a number pad. You can also set up an office space with an external keyboard, mouse, and monitor.

Connect an External Monitor

1. Make sure that your external monitor can be connected to your laptop. Typical connections include a VGA or DVI connection.

2. Right-click your desktop and choose Personalize⇨ Display Settings to see the Display Settings dialog box, shown in Figure 10-7.

3. If you want the external monitor to *mirror* your normal laptop screen (to show the same things on it), click the screen labeled 2 and specify the same settings as your laptop screen.

4. If you want to use the external monitor as an extension of your main screen, select the screen labeled 2 and select the Extend the Desktop onto This Monitor check box, as shown in Figure 10-8. Leave your laptop monitor as the main monitor.

 Even if you don't make the right connection immediately, don't fret and return either the laptop or the monitor. Adapters to convert VGA connections to DVI connections (and vice versa) are available.

 A mirrored display is a good option for external LCD projectors in presentation situations.

 An extended desktop lets you use the external screen for other windows. You can type a paper on one screen, for example, and use the other screen for reference material (or to control your media player and watch TV).

Figure 10-7: Your monitor settings

Figure 10-8: Extending your desktop to an external monitor

Connect and Use an External Hard Drive

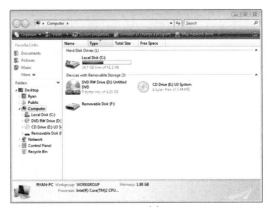

Figure 10-9: Locating your external drive

1. Connect the external drive to your computer. If it has an external power source, turn on the drive.

2. As shown in Figure 10-9, your drive is accessible by clicking the Start button and selecting Computer. In this case, the external drive is available as drive F.

3. The external drive can now be used as just another hard drive on your laptop. You can save, move, or delete files as you would do on any other drive.

4. To remove an external hard drive from your computer, click the Safely Remove Hardware icon in the lower-right corner of your desktop to open the Safely Remove Hardware dialog box, shown in Figure 10-10.

5. Select the drive you want to remove and click Stop. Wait until you receive notice that it's okay to remove the device and then do so.

Figure 10-10: Removing an external drive

 Depending on what you store on your hard drive (music, pictures, documents, and other types of files), you may see other options in the AutoPlay window when the drive is connected. You can access files from either the AutoPlay window or an Explorer window.

 Smaller flash drives are useful for transporting files from one location to another, whereas larger hard disc drives are useful for long-term file storage.

 Always stop a drive before you disconnect it or turn it off. You can corrupt your files or damage your hardware if you fail to do so.

 All hard drives eventually fail — it's just a matter of time. It might take a few days or even a few years. If you absolutely need to keep certain data safe, burn it to a CD or DVD and keep it in a safe place as a "just in case" backup.

Connect a Scanner or Camera

1. Install any software that came with your device.

    This task applies to only the Business, Enterprise, and Ultimate versions of Vista.

2. Connect your device and turn on the power.

3. To confirm that your scanner is connected, choose Start⇨ Control Panel⇨Scanners and Cameras to display the Scanners and Cameras dialog box, shown in Figure 10-11.

4. To scan a document or pictures, choose Start⇨Control Panel and select Scan a Document or Picture under the Scanners and Cameras heading.

5. Insert the document you want to scan into your scanner.

6. Click the New Scan button, shown in Figure 10-12.

7. Preview the scan and determine your scan settings; then press Scan to create the file. Save it to the location of your choice.

8. A connected camera either uses its software to transfer files or acts as a hard drive to move files to your laptop. Follow the manufacturer instructions to move the files.

    Cameras and scanners often come with different versions of photo manipulation software, often in trial or "consumer" versions that lack the features of their full-fledged brethren. If you don't need it, don't install it.

    Some software, such as Adobe Photoshop or Acrobat, allows you to scan documents and pictures from inside the program. In this case, use whichever program you feel more comfortable with.

Figure 10-11: Scanners and cameras

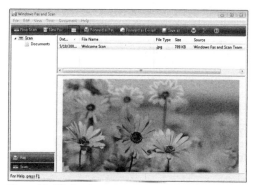

Figure 10-12: Creating a new scan

Connect and Use a Portable Media Device

1. Install any software that came with your device.

2. Connect the device to your laptop and turn it on.

3. Open the appropriate software and start copying or syncing files to your player.

4. To disconnect your device, close the software and click the Safely Remove Hardware icon to stop the player.

 More than any other device, a portable media player (such as the iPod) is built to interface with a specific piece of software (such as iTunes). You *must* load that software first.

Connect a Game Controller

1. Load any software that came with the controller.

2. Connect the game controller to the laptop by using a USB cable.

3. Click Start⟷Control Panel⟷Hardware and Sound⟷Game Controllers to open the Game Controllers dialog box, shown in Figure 10-13.

4. Select the controller you want to use and click Properties to set it up.

 Even if it's a wireless controller, it probably has a USB adapter. Controllers can also connect by way of a Bluetooth connection.

 Different games also have menus inside them to further refine your game controller.

Figure 10-13: The Game Controllers dialog box

Make a Bluetooth Connection

1. Make sure that the Bluetooth adapter on your laptop is turned on.

2. Turn on the Bluetooth function for your remote device. Make sure that it's set for Discoverable.

3. Choose Start⇨Control Panel⇨Hardware and Sound⇨ Bluetooth Devices to see the Bluetooth Devices dialog box, shown in Figure 10-14.

4. Click Add to have the Add Bluetooth Device Wizard help you search for available devices, as shown in Figure 10-15.

5. Set up the devices, depending on the manufacturer instructions and properties.

 Bluetooth can be used to connect wireless keyboards and mice, cell phones, and other devices. How you set it up depends on what it does.

 Connect only to devices you know and trust. Connecting to random devices can give other people control over your laptop and its contents.

Figure 10-14: Listing Bluetooth devices

Figure 10-15: Searching for Bluetooth devices

Making Your Own Media

*L*aptops may be the computers of choice for business travelers and other job functions. However, more and more people are taking advantage of the increased power and flexibility of today's laptops and are using them as the main machines for work or entertainment. Heck, even that weary business traveler needs a little relaxation now and then.

Your Vista laptop includes plenty of tools for both creating and playing audio and video. By following a few quick tips, you'll be on your way to turning your computer into a personal jukebox or entertainment center. Have fun!

Chapter 11

Get ready to . . .

Rip a CD

1. Insert an audio CD into your laptop's optical drive.

2. In the AutoPlay window, shown in Figure 11-1, choose Rip Music from CD. You can also access this option by opening Windows Media Player and clicking the Rip tab.

    Plenty of media players are available that can rip audio from a CD, and you can choose whichever player you want to use. However, because Windows Media Player comes bundled with Vista, I stick with that one.

3. Windows Media Player automatically rips songs from the CD and places them in your My Music folder, as shown in Figure 11-2.

    Connect your laptop to the Internet before ripping audio from a CD. You can create the tracks in any case, but Windows Media Player pulls all the album information automatically during the ripping process, giving you more control over how your music is organized.

4. After the tracks have been ripped, you can play back tracks at any time by selecting the track and pressing the Play button (the big button with the triangle in the middle) at the bottom of the player.

    Windows Media Player rips audio by default to 128 Kbps Windows Media Audio files (.wma). You can change the file type to MP3, Windows Media Lossless, or WAV files of different types by clicking the Rip tab and selecting More Options. Remember, better audio quality means larger files, and some media players may require different file formats.

Figure 11-1: The CD AutoPlay menu

Figure 11-2: Ripping tracks from a CD

Create a Music Library

1. Click Start⇨All Programs and select Windows Media Player.

2. Click the Library tab to see the view shown in Figure 11-3.

3. Click the Library tab again to see the menu options and choose Add To Library.

4. Click the Advanced Options button to extend the Add to Library dialog box, shown in Figure 11-4.

5. Audio files stored in your personal folders are automatically added to your library. Choose Add to bring in additional folders or click Remove to take out other folders.

6. Use the columns on the left side of the media player to sort through the tracks you want to play. You can sort tracks based on different criteria:

Recently Added	Genre
Artist	Year
Album	Rating
Songs	

 You can add ratings to your track by clicking the number of stars next to the track. After you rate the tracks, you can separate your favorite songs from everything else in your library.

7. Use the controls at the bottom of the media player window to start, stop, and move forward and backward through the available tracks.

8. Use the two buttons on the far left end of the player controls to specify whether the tracks are shuffled randomly during playback or whether you want them to repeat.

 Turning on both the Shuffle and Random functions is a good way to simulate your own, personal radio station. Remember to turn off these functions if you want to stick with the traditional album format, though. It can be jarring to move from a slow symphony to your hard rock favorite.

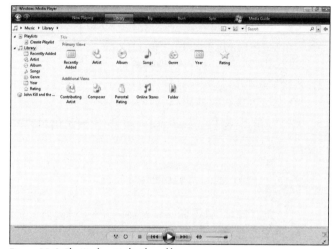

Figure 11-3: The Windows Media Player library

Figure 11-4: Adding music folders to your Windows Media Player library

Create a Playlist

1. Open Windows Media Player and click the Create Playlist link on the left side of the player.

2. Type the name of your new playlist and press Enter. Click the playlist to view the screen shown in Figure 11-5.

3. Click the Songs link on the left side of the playlist to view the songs in your library.

4. Click and drag the songs you want on your new playlist to the right side of the player, as shown in Figure 11-6.

5. Click the Save Playlist button in the lower-right corner to save the songs in your playlist.

    You can reorder the songs in your playlist by clicking and dragging them either before or after other tracks.

    You can include the same song on multiple playlists, if you want. You need only one copy on your computer, though.

6. Double-click the playlist in the left column to start playing the songs on the list. You can use the playback controls to skip tracks or stop playback.

    The Shuffle and Repeat commands still work while you're playing back a playlist. They skip and shuffle only the songs in the playlist, not in the entire library.

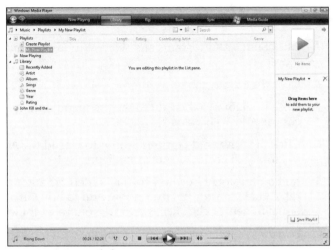

Figure 11-5: My new playlist

Figure 11-6: Placing songs on the playlist

Connect a Portable Media Player

1. Install on your laptop any software or drivers included with your player.

    Different players interact with computers in different ways with different software. In this case, you're looking at devices that sync directly with Windows Media Player. Follow the instructions for your personal media player, and make sure that it specifically syncs directly to Windows Media Player, if that's what you want.

2. Open Windows Media Player and click the Sync tab (see Figure 11-7).

3. Drag the song titles and album covers to the right side of the player to sync to the player (see Figure 11-8).

4. Connect your portable media player to the computer by following the device's instructions.

5. After Windows Media Player recognizes your device, click the Start Sync button in the lower-right corner to copy the files from your laptop to your device.

6. Follow your player's instructions to disconnect the portable media player from your laptop after the transfer is finished.

    Wait until all transfers are finished to disconnect your device properly. Failure to do so means that (at best) not all your files are coped and (at worst) you can damage your player or laptop.

Figure 11-7: The Sync tab

Figure 11-8: Syncing songs and albums to your player

Burn a Music CD

1. Insert a blank CD-R into your CD burner.

 CD-RW discs might not play as well in standard CD players, so stick to CD-Rs in this case.

2. Open Windows Media Player and click the Burn tab (see Figure 11-9). You can also access this view by clicking the Burn Music to CD link in the AutoPlay window that pops up when you insert a blank CD.

3. Drag songs from the library over to the right column of the Windows Media Player. You see the time remaining in the upper-right corner of the player window.

 The laptop burns the tracks in the order you drag them to the list. You can also choose to burn a playlist that you already created.

 Double-check all song titles when you're done to make sure that they're in the order you want. After a CD-R is burned, you can't undo it.

4. After you drag over all the songs you want to burn, or after you run out of space and time, click the Start Burn button to burn the CD, as shown in Figure 11-10.

5. After the disc finishes burning, you can safely eject it from your laptop and play it in a normal CD player, if it doesn't happen automatically.

Figure 11-9: The Burn tab

Figure 11-10: Burning a CD

Import a Photo

1. If required, install any software that came with your camera.

    Your camera might not require any software to transfer files to your laptop — some show up as external hard drives and allow you to move files just like another disc. Always check and follow your manufacturer's instructions.

2. Connect your camera or memory card to your laptop and click the Import Pictures link in the AutoPlay window, shown in Figure 11-11. You use the AutoPlay function to tag photos with text descriptions as they're copied.

3. Click Start⇨All Programs⇨Windows Photo Gallery to open and view pictures, as shown in Figure 11-12.

4. You can add photos from other sources, such as downloads or other discs, by clicking and dragging photos from your folders into the Windows Photo Gallery.

5. Use the links in the left column to navigate the photos in your gallery. As with your music files, you can rate and tag them for easier sorting. Click the Create a New Tag link on the left side to add information to a photo (such as the subject, where it was taken, or a specific event).

    Adding tags and being as descriptive as possible helps you sort individual photos more quickly, especially when your library grows too large to search easily. Tags and descriptive names are also easier to recognize than DSC-1101, for example, and similar names assigned by some digital cameras.

Figure 11-11: Importing photos

Figure 11-12: Windows Photo Gallery

Start a Photo Slide Show

1. Navigate to the folder containing the photos you want to display.

    Creating a quick and easy slide show is just one of many good reasons to keep your photos organized in separate folders with descriptive terms. This type of organization helps you include only the photos you want in your slide show.

2. Click the Slide Show button in the menu bar to begin your slide show (see Figure 11-13).

3. The show begins automatically and occupies your entire screen. Move the cursor to see the following controls on the control panel at the bottom of the figure (see Figure 11-14).

   • **Themes menu:** Change how photos are displayed, including black-and-white and sepia and different movements and transitions.

   • **Play controls:** Start, pause, and skip photos. These controls are in the middle of the toolbar.

   • **Gear icon:** Change the speed, shuffle, and repeat settings of the slide show.

4. To leave the slide show, click Exit or press the Esc key on your laptop keyboard.

    This feature is handy for displaying photos at gatherings or sales presentations either on your laptop screen or on an external projector.

Figure 11-13: The Slide Show button

Figure 11-14: Controlling the slide show

Resize a Photo

1. Click Start⇨All Programs⇨Accessories and select Paint.

2. In Paint, choose File⇨Open and navigate to the photo you want to resize, as shown in Figure 11-15.

3. With the photo open, choose Image⇨Resize/Skew to display the Resize and Skew dialog box, shown in Figure 11-16.

4. Enter the percentage you want to shrink or enlarge the photo and click OK.

 Resize the vertical and horizontal aspects by the same percentage to keep the photo from looking warped.

 Start with a large photo and shrink it to the correct size (rather than start with a small photo and try to enlarge it to what you need). You end up with better detail and quality if you start with a larger photo than you need.

 Paint is a simple but effective tool for manipulating photo sizes. Other programs are available that do more than just adjust photos, including the venerable Adobe Photoshop and the free, open source GIMP (GNU Image Manipulation Program) available at the site www.gimp.org.

Figure 11-15: Opening a photo

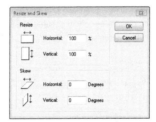

Figure 11-16: Resizing a photo

Import Video into Windows Movie Maker

1. Install any software included with your digital video camera.

    Depending on your camera, you may not need any additional software to move video from your camera to your computer. Follow the manufacturers' instructions.

2. Use your camera's software or Vista's AutoPlay function to transfer the video to your computer.

    Each device has its own way of bringing video to your laptop. You may have to use software, or you may be able to just drag and drop video files, as you can with other documents and files. Again, refer to your instructions.

3. Click Start➪All Programs➪Windows Movie Maker to open the program, shown in Figure 11-17.

4. Click the Videos link in the Import section on the left side of the screen, and navigate to the location of your video clip, as shown in Figure 11-18.

5. Select the video you want and click Import. The video is imported into Windows Movie Maker.

    After a video is imported, you're ready to change the length, cut, and make other adjustments to the clip.

    Use the other links in the Import section to bring photos and music into Windows Movie Maker.

Figure 11-17: Windows Movie Maker

Figure 11-18: Importing video into Windows Movie Maker

Create a Video Project

1. Import into Windows Movie Maker all the video, photos, and music you want to use in your project.

2. Click View➪Timeline to show the Timeline view of Windows Movie Maker.

     Timeline view lets you control the length of time that your still photos are displayed and add audio. If you want to just drag video clips into a certain order and create your movie, stay in Storyboard view.

3. Drag the video clips into the timeline at the bottom of Windows Movie Maker, as shown in Figure 11-19.

4. Move the clips around until you have your order and playtimes set.

5. You can add effects to the video, create transitions from one clip to the next, and add titles and credits using the links on the left side of Windows Movie Maker.

6. After everything is ready, choose how you want to publish your video (as a video file on your computer, as a DVD, or other options) and click the option at the bottom of the left column. In this example, you publish the video as a file to your laptop.

7. In the dialog box that opens when you publish the video, choose the name and location of your video file and click Next.

8. In the Publish Movie dialog box, shown in Figure 11-20, choose the settings for your video and click Publish.

     Unless you're familiar with digital video terminology, stick with the default settings. Smaller videos are easier to move, but they have lower quality.

9. After your laptop runs through the publishing process, your video is in the location you chose.

Figure 11-19: The Windows Movie Maker timeline

Figure 11-20: Default settings usually work well

Burn Files to a CD or DVD

1. Insert a blank, recordable CD into your CD burner.

2. Either select the Burn Files to Disc command from the AutoPlay window or click Start and select Computer from the right column of the Start menu to navigate to the blank CD.

3. Type the title of the CD you're creating in Figure 11-21.

4. Click the Advanced tab to choose the type of format you want to use on your CD. The Live File System option lets you add and change files later, and the Mastered option completes the CD when the burning process is done.

 If you plan to transfer this CD to other computers, select the Mastered option. The Live File System option doesn't transfer well to other computers.

5. Drag the files you want to burn to the disc, as shown in Figure 11-22.

6. Click Burn to Disc in the menu bar, set the disc title (again) and the burn speed, and click Next.

 Unless you experience problems, leave the burn speed alone.

7. After the disc is complete, you can either burn another copy or complete the project. Make your selection and click Finish.

Figure 11-21: The burned CD format

Figure 11-22: Burning files to disc

Part III
Expanding Your Network

The 5th Wave — By Rich Tennant

"You ever notice how much more streaming media there is than there used to be?"

Keeping Yourself Wired

As useful as your laptop is, it can do only so much on its own. Whether it's for your business or your personal entertainment, much of your laptop's functionality depends on connecting to the Internet or to other computers. The most secure way is to use a wired network, where your laptop is connected by a physical cable to a network.

This chapter helps you route your high-speed connection to the computers in your home and keep everything safe and secure. After you finish, you can access whatever you need with a simple and quick connection.

Chapter 12

Get ready to . . .

Physically Connect Your Computer or Router

Modem

Figure 12-1: Connecting a high-speed modem to a computer

1. Connect an Ethernet cable to your cable, satellite, or DSL modem.

2. If you're just using your laptop, connect the Ethernet cable directly to your computer, as shown in Figure 12-1.

3. If you want to use multiple computers from the same modem connection, connect the Ethernet cable from the modem to a router.

    A *router* is a device that splits a single network connection among several devices on a network, including computers, printers, and other network-capable devices. You have to buy one (most service providers don't include one with their services), but it's the only way to go for home networks.

4. Connect several Ethernet cables to the outgoing ports on the router.

5. Connect the cables to all the computers you want to use, as shown in Figure 12-2.

    You always need a high-speed connection to use a router. If you're still suffering with a dial-up connection, you can use only one computer on one phone line at a time.

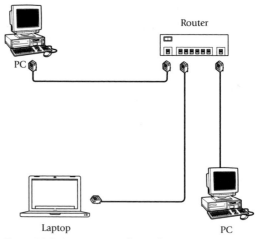

Figure 12-2: Using a router with several computers

Access Your Router's Controls

1. Make sure that your computer is connected to the router.

2. Open your Web browser and enter the address provided by your router's manufacturer.

3. In the Connect To dialog box that opens (see Figure 12-3), type the default username and password provided by your router's manufacturer.

4. Your Web browser shows the initial settings for your router, as shown in Figure 12-4. You can access the settings from this page each time you log in.

     The router address consists of four groups of numbers separated by periods, such as 192.168.1.1. The address follows the same format as other Web addresses, but can be accessed only by devices on your network.

5. Refer to your router's instructions for any additional setup information for first-time users.

     One of the first actions you should take with your new router is to change the default username and password. Leaving this information unchanged means that anybody who has the instruction manual to this router (easily available on the Internet) can gain access to your router's settings.

     Each router has its own interface and installation instructions, but the instructions listed in this section generally work for all models. Check the manufacturer's instructions for specific information about your particular brand of router.

Figure 12-3: Logging in to your router

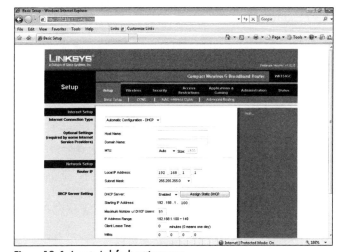

Figure 12-4: A router's default settings page

Set Up Your Router

1. Access your router's settings using the default username and password.

2. Change the default username and password so that they're unique. As demonstrated in Figure 12-5, the password is "hidden" so that other people can't see what you type.

3. Change the date-and-time settings on the router, as shown in Figure 12-6.

4. Check with your Internet service provider (ISP) and change the settings according to its specifications.

     Most of the time, your router's default settings (usually, an automatic connection method known as DHCP) work just fine. You may have to make some adjustments, though. Check with your provider to be sure.

5. Restart the router, if necessary.

     Routers are easy to set up and then leave alone — that's what they're made to do. However, if you start having problems with your network connection, you might have to restart your router, just as you would do with your computer. Either unplug the power cord and replace it, or use your router's power switch, if it has one.

6. Check to ensure that all devices hooked to the router have active connections to the Internet.

Figure 12-5: Changing your router's password

Figure 12-6: Changing the router's date and time

Filter the Computers That Can Use Your Network

1. Click the Start button and choose Computer.

2. Type **cmd** in the field at the top of the window.

3. In the command line window that opens, type **getmac** and press Return. The result is similar to the one shown in Figure 12-7.

4. Write down the numbers you see in this format: XX:XX:XX:XX:XX:XX. This number is the MAC address of your computer's network card.

5. Log in to your router and go to the MAC address filtering settings.

6. Set the router to allow only computers listed in the MAC list, as shown in Figure 12-8.

    Each network device on your computer has its own MAC address, so you can have three addresses (wireless, wired, and Bluetooth) for each system. Be sure to register all of them.

7. Enter the address of your computer, and repeat for all computers that will access your router.

    Because wired routers require a physical connection, this step is more valuable for wireless routers than wired. If you're not always sure who will connect to your router, though, it's a valuable security measure.

Figure 12-7: Determining your computer's MAC address

Figure 12-8: Setting the router's MAC filtering

Set Up Your Router's Firewall

1. Access your router's settings page.

2. Navigate to the Firewall section and select Enabled SPI Firewall, as shown in Figure 12-9.

     The firewall blocks unauthorized access to the devices and computers on your network. Always leave the firewall on your router turned on.

     Windows Vista has a built-in firewall for your computer, but it doesn't protect any other network devices, so you should leave both of them on.

3. Save your settings immediately.

4. Navigate to your firewall's port settings and set up any exceptions, as dictated by the programs you use. See Figure 12-10 for an example.

     Most basic Web services are enabled by default on routers. Make only the changes specified by the programs you use.

5. Save the settings and restart the router, as necessary.

6. Make sure that your laptop still has Internet access and that all programs and devices are working normally.

Figure 12-9: Enabling the firewall

| Port Range Forwarding | | | | | |
Application Name	Start – End Port	Protocol	To IP Address	Enabled
DNS ▼	53 – 53	☐ TCP ☑ UDP	192.168.1.1	☐
Finger ▼	79 – 79	☑ TCP ☐ UDP	192.168.1.1	☐
FTP ▼	20 – 21	☑ TCP ☐ UDP	192.168.1.1	☐
POP3 ▼	110 – 110	☑ TCP ☐ UDP	192.168.1.1	☐
SMTP ▼	25 – 25	☑ TCP ☐ UDP	192.168.1.1	☐
snmp	161 – 161	☐ TCP ☑ UDP	192.168.1.1	☐
telnet	23 – 23	☑ TCP ☐ UDP	192.168.1.1	☐
tftp	69 – 69	☐ TCP ☑ UDP	192.168.1.1	☐
web	80 – 80	☑ TCP ☐ UDP	192.168.1.1	☐

Figure 12-10: Allowing services through the firewall

Cutting the Cords

*P*art of the reason you purchased a laptop is most likely that you want to be free and mobile. You probably need to take your computer with you and to be able to access all its functions anywhere you are (even if that anywhere is just down the hall from your home office, on the couch). By using a wireless network, you can access everything you use, just as though cables are connected wherever you are — except, of course, that you won't trip over them.

In this chapter, you discover how to set up your own home wireless network and customize it to your needs. You also find out how to secure the network from unwanted attention. You don't want just anybody plugging into your virtual cables, do you?

Chapter 13

Get ready to . . .

Set Up Your Wireless Router

1. Connect the wireless router to your cable modem and power it on.

2. Connect your computer to the wireless router by way of a cable.

    Always keep a cable ready to connect to your wireless router. That way, if you accidentally change a setting on the router that prevents you from accessing your wireless network, you have a backup connection ready to change it back.

3. Access the settings on your wireless router and select the Wireless Network settings, shown in Figure 13-1.

4. Name your wireless network by typing a name in the Wireless Network Name (SSID) field.

5. Change the channel of your network broadcast in the Wireless Channel drop-down list, as shown in Figure 13-2.

    Wireless routers usually default to Channel 6, which means that you may see some interference if several wireless routers are in your area. Changing the default channel helps clear up the confusion.

6. Choose whether you want to broadcast the name of your network.

    Not broadcasting the name of your network keeps casual observers from finding it, but it also complicates your access to the network. If you're having problems accessing your network because the name isn't being broadcast, leave the broadcast on.

7. Save your settings and try to access your wireless network after you disconnect the cable.

Figure 13-1: Wireless router settings

Figure 13-2: Changing the router's broadcast channel

Choose the Speed of Your Network

1. Examine your wireless devices and determine whether they function on 802.11b, 802.11g, or 802.11n.

 The numbers in front of the letters *b*, *g*, or *n* simply indicate that the network is wireless network, so you don't have to pay much attention to them. Just remember that as the letters progress through the alphabet, the network speed gets faster. Devices can go only as fast as their highest letter, though. A B device, for example, goes only that fast, even on a faster network.

Figure 13-3: Wireless network speed choices

2. After you determine which speeds your devices require, access your router's Wireless Network settings, as shown in Figure 13-3.

 You can find the speed of a wireless device by checking its manufacturer's instructions. The most common speed at the time this book was printed was G. Older devices may still use B, and a small but growing number of devices using N have been rolled out.

3. If you have only B devices, set the network speed for B or B-Only.

4. If you have only G devices, set the network speed for G or G-only.

5. If you have only N devices (and both your laptop and router can handle it), set the speed for N or N-only.

6. If you have a mixture of devices, set the speed to Mixed.

 A mixed signal allows both B and G devices to function on the same network, except that the G devices don't move as fast as they do a G-only network. This setting may affect large downloads or heavy gaming traffic, for example.

7. Save your settings and make sure that your wireless devices can still access the network.

Add a Wireless Access Point

1. Power on your laptop's wireless access point, and plug it in to your router or put it in the location where you want to use it. Figure 13-4 shows you how to connect the wireless access point (WAP) to the router, and Figure 13-5 shows you how to connect it as a booster.

     A wireless access point can make a wired router broadcast a wireless signal, or it can be used to boost and extend the range of your current wireless router.

2. Access the access point's settings as described in the manufacturer's instructions.

3. Choose how you want the WAP to broadcast — as a primary access point or as a booster.

4. Set up the wireless access point as you would a wireless router.

     Be sure to enable all security functions on both your router and your wireless access point, just to make sure that there's not a hole in your laptop's network security.

5. Save the settings on the access point.

6. Try to access the wireless network by using your laptop.

Router   Wireless access point   Laptop

Figure 13-4: A wireless access point connected to a router

Wireless router   Wireless access point   Laptop

Figure 13-5: A wireless access point rebroadcasting a router's signal

Encrypt Your Network Traffic

1. Access your wireless router and navigate to the Wireless Security tab.

2. Choose the type of wireless security you want to use, as shown in Figure 13-6.

    If all your devices allow it, use WPA2 wireless security rather than lesser or older protocols. WPA2 provides better security to home users than other protocols do, although older devices might not be able to handle WPA2.

3. Enter your passphrase in the Passphrase field, as shown in Figure 13-7.

    The best password or passphrase isn't easy to guess, and it involves mixed characters, such as capital letters, numbers, spaces, and symbols. Try to use a random string of characters. (Some wireless routers generate the string for you.)

4. Save your settings.

5. Reconnect your laptop to your wireless network and enter a new password or passphrase.

    Make all these changes while your laptop is connected to the router with a cable. If you accidentally change or forget a setting, you still can gain access by using a physical connection.

Figure 13-6: Choosing an encryption protocol

Figure 13-7: Entering a passphrase

Connect Your Laptop to a Wireless Network

1. Click Start and select Connect To.

2. In the dialog box shown in Figure 13-8, select the network you want to connect to.

 Connect only to a wireless network you trust. Connecting to unknown networks endangers your laptop and the data that's on it.

3. If the network is secured, enter the password or passphrase and press Enter.

4. If the network is hidden, you can set up a manual connection by clicking the Start button and choosing Connect To➪Set Up a Connection or Network➪ Manually Connect to a Wireless Network.

5. In the Manually Connect to a Wireless Network dialog box, shown in Figure 13-9, enter the necessary network (like the network's SSID and password) information and click Next.

6. Check your laptop's network connection to make sure that you can use your network normally.

 You can also see wireless activity in an icon in the lower-right corner of the screen. Look for the icon that looks like two overlapping computer screens, and right-click it to change your current network settings.

 To improve your laptop's battery life, leave your wireless card turned off if you're not using it.

Figure 13-8: Selecting a wireless network

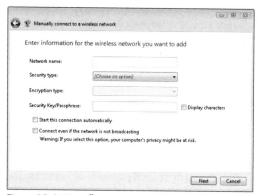

Figure 13-9: Manually setting up a wireless network

Share and Share Alike

A s powerful as today's laptops are, part of that power relies on connections to other devices. Your laptop can use larger hard drives, different devices, and even other computers. Even if a device is physically linked to another computer, your laptop can still use it.

Using wired and wireless network connections, you can create a web of storage and access that makes any device usable by any computer. All it takes is a few clicks of the mouse, and you're on your way to making the links you need. This chapter shows you how to set up your own shared network of connections and devices.

Chapter 14

Get ready to . . .

Set Security Permissions for Drives, Files, and Folders

1. Select the drive, file, or folder you want to modify and right-click it.

2. Choose Properties and select the Security tab in the Properties dialog box shown in Figure 14-1.

3. Each group or user listed in the top section has different access to the selected drive, file, or folder. Click the appropriate group name to see the permissions listed in the bottom section.

 Administrative users have access to all files and folders on a specific computer. Be sure to limit the amount of administrative users on your computer to just those that truly need it (not your kids, for example).

4. To edit permissions for a specific user or group, select them in the top section and click the Edit button.

5. Select the check boxes for the permissions you want to enable for that drive, file, or folder, as shown in Figure 14-2. Write permissions allow them to add information to a file, Modify allows them to change information in the file, and Full Control allows them to move or delete the file itself.

 The permissions shown in Figure 14-2 are standard for nonadministrative users. If they don't need permission, don't give it to them.

Figure 14-1: Security properties

Figure 14-2: Changing security permissions

Share Individual Files and Folders

1. Navigate to the file or folder you want to share.

2. Right-click the file or folder and choose Share to open the File Sharing dialog box, shown in Figure 14-3.

3. Click the drop-down list near the top and select a user to share your information with. Click the Add button to add that person to the list.

4. Click the arrow next to the user's name to set that person's permissions, as shown in Figure 14-4.

5. Click the Share button to make the file or folder available to the selected users.

6. After the sharing process is completed, the screen displays a link to the file or folder. Send that link to the appropriate users so that they can paste it into the Explorer window to access it.

 You can also place a shortcut to the file or folder on the user's desktop to provide easier access.

 Shared files and folders are available only when the laptop is turned on and connected to that specific network. Any other location renders the file or folder inaccessible.

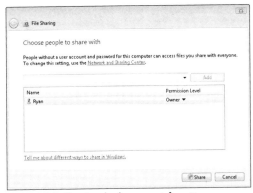

Figure 14-3: Choosing who shares your information

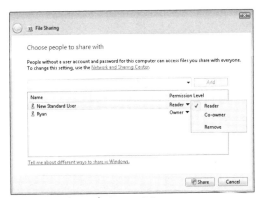

Figure 14-4: Setting sharing permissions

Share Entire Drives on Your Computer

1. Click Start and select Computer.

2. Right-click the drive you want to share and choose Share.

3. On the Sharing tab, shown in Figure 14-5, click Advanced Sharing; then select the Share This Folder check box, as shown in Figure 14-6.

    Make sure that you want everything on that drive to be accessible.

4. Click the Permissions button to specify whom you want to access the share and what you want that person to be able to do.

5. Click OK to finish the sharing process.

Figure 14-5: Drive sharing properties

Figure 14-6: Creating a share

Share a Printer

1. Click Start and select Control Panel.

2. Look in the Hardware and Sound section and click the Printer link.

3. Right-click the printer you want to share and choose Sharing to display the Properties dialog box shown in Figure 14-7.

4. Click the Change Sharing Options button and select the Share This Printer check box, as shown in Figure 14-8.

 Make sure the printer you want to share is on a computer that's turned on most of the time. When the computer is turned off, that printer isn't available.

 That printer is available only when you're connected to your home network. Even if you're connected to the Internet at another location, the printer isn't available.

Figure 14-7: Sharing a printer

Figure 14-8: Changing a printer's sharing status

Set Up a Shared Network Connection for Two or More Computers

1. Click the Start button and select Network, and then select Network and Sharing Center from the top menu bar.

2. Select the Set Up a Connection or Network command under Tasks in the left column to see the Set Up a Connection or Network dialog box, shown in Figure 14-9.

3. Click Set Up a Wireless Ad Hoc Network and click Next.

4. Enter a network name, security type, and passphrase for your ad hoc network, as shown in Figure 14-10. Click Next to create the network.

 To keep your data safe, use the strongest level of security possible on your ad hoc network. Remember that WPA is stronger and preferable to WEP.

 Never connect to an ad hoc network you're not familiar with. It's a huge security risk.

5. Click Share an Internet Connection on an Ad Hoc Network to allow others to use your network connection.

6. You're notified when the network is created. Click Close and connect another computer to the network.

Figure 14-9: Choosing a connection

Figure 14-10: Creating an ad hoc network

Create a Shared Media Folder for Multiple Computers

1. Click the Start button and select Network, and then select Network and Sharing Center from the top menu bar.

2. Under Sharing and Discovery, click the Media Sharing arrow button and click Change to see the Media Sharing dialog box, shown in Figure 14-11.

3. Select the Share My Media check box and Click OK.

4. In the Media Sharing dialog box, select the names of users you want to allow access to and click Allow.

5. Click the Settings button to determine which media you share, as shown in Figure 14-12. Click OK when you're finished.

6. Click OK to share media.

7. To access the shared media from another account, open Windows Media Player and choose Library⊅Media Sharing. Select the Find Media That Others Are Sharing check box and click OK. Available shares are automatically connected.

 Make sure that only the media you want to share is made available. Carefully select the playlists and ratings you want to share.

Figure 14-11: Sharing your media

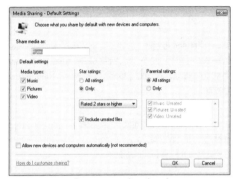

Figure 14-12: Choosing your shared media

Connect to a Remote Server

1. Click the Start button and select Computer.

2. Click the Map Network Drive button at the top of the menu bar.

3. In the Map Network Drive dialog box, shown in Figure 14-13, enter the drive letter and the location of the drive. You can also click the Connect to a Web Site That You Can Use link to access an FTP server over your Internet connection.

 The drive letter and location, as well as any Web server addresses, should be provided to you by the owner of the drive. If you created the shared drive earlier, that process gave you all the necessary information.

 No two drives can have the same drive letter — you can't connect to one of them in any case. To avoid confusion, try assigning remote drive letters from later in the alphabet.

4. To make this connection permanent, select the Reconnect at Logon check box.

5. If the drive has different security permissions than your current login allows, click the Different User Name link. You're asked to enter the appropriate username and password.

6. After you enter all your information, click the Finish button. The drive should be displayed automatically, and you can access it by using the Computer icon, as shown in Figure 14-14.

Figure 14-13: Connecting to a remote drive

Figure 14-14: The mapped network drive

Use Public Folders

1. Click the Start button and select Control Panel.

2. Under the Network and Internet section, click Set Up File Sharing and select the Public Folder Sharing option to see the Network and Sharing Center, shown in Figure 14-15.

3. By default, the option is turned off. However, you can choose to allow users with accounts on your computer to use the folder and its contents, or you can let anybody on your network manipulate (change or rename, for example) them. Choose the option you want and click the Apply button.

Figure 14-15: Public folder sharing

 Using public folders is a useful way to share information with others without granting them access to your personal folders and telling them where information in your account is located.

 If you choose to allow anybody on your network to have access to your public folders, remember to put in there only the information you want to share. Your folders are available to *anybody* connected to your network.

4. Navigate to your public folders by clicking the Start button and selecting Computer. Click the Public link to see the screen shown in Figure 14-16.

5. Drop whatever information you want to share in the appropriate public folder. That folder is accessible to others on your network.

6. To connect to a public folder, map the drive, as explained in the earlier "Connect to a Remote Server" task.

Figure 14-16: Your public folders

Home and Away Games

Chapter

15

Your home wireless network can be a safe haven for your laptop, but the time comes when you have to take your computer to the outside world. Plenty of networks are out there for you to use, ranging from your company's network to the connection down at the coffee shop or the network in the airport's waiting area. Your laptop is perfectly capable of using any of these connections, given the right information.

This chapter explains how to use those network connections, and how to keep your computer safe while using them. You don't have the same control over other networks as you do at home, but you can keep your laptop safe while you're using them.

Get ready to . . .

Evaluate the Safety of Networks That Your Laptop Finds

1. Click Start➪Connect To or right-click the icon shown in Figure 15-1 and choose Connect to a Network.

2. Look at the available network properties: The name of the network is listed on the left, the type of network is shown in the center, and the strength of the network is shown on the right (see Figure 15-2).

3. If the location you're in specifies the name of a network, choose that one (and only that one).

4. Unsecured networks allow all network traffic, and the information you send and receive can be seen by other computers. Choose a secured network if possible (and if the location gives you the password to use).

 Avoid connecting to an unsecured wireless network that you're not familiar with. It might be an open network provided by a friendly household, but it can also present problems with unsecured data.

5. Don't connect to ad hoc networks unless you're absolutely sure what's at the other end. This type of connection makes a direct link between your laptop and another computer.

 Beware of networks with names like Free Airport Wireless. Often, these are ad hoc networks set up to lure unfamiliar users to connect their computers. After you complete the tasks in this chapter, you'll know better than to use them.

The wireless-connection icon

Figure 15-1: The wireless-connection icon

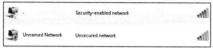

Figure 15-2: Properties of a wireless network

Use a VPN to Encrypt Network Traffic

1. Click Start⇨Network⇨Network and Sharing Center⇨ Set Up a Connection or Network.

2. In the dialog box shown in Figure 15-3, select Connect to a Workplace and click Next.

3. Select the VPN option.

 A *virtual private network*, or *VPN*, helps keep your data safe in the wild by encrypting the traffic that your laptop sends and receives over a public network.

4. Enter the server information and network name provided by your business or VPN service, as shown in Figure 15-4.

 If you're not employed by or part of a business that provides VPN service, you can sign up with a commercial provider. If you travel often, consider purchasing this type of account to keep your important data secure and safe.

5. Select the check boxes at the bottom of the dialog box as directed by your VPN provider and then click Next.

6. Enter your username, password, and domain information as directed and click Create.

7. To activate your VPN, click Start⇨Connect To and double-click your VPN connection.

 Different types of VPN connections exist, and your company or service provider may require you to make additional changes. Their instructions describe how to modify connections from there. You can access these settings by clicking Start⇨Connect To and right-clicking the VPN connection. Choose Properties to see additional settings.

Figure 15-3: Connecting to your workplace

Figure 15-4: Entering VPN information

Secure Your Laptop for Use on Unfamiliar Networks

1. Click Start⇨Network⇨Network Sharing Center.

2. In the window shown in Figure 15-5, look at all the sharing services that are enabled and decide whether you truly need them.

3. Click the arrow button next to any unnecessary services (on the far right end of the window) to turn them off.

    If you leave sharing services enabled, connect only to sources you trust. Remember that you're still establishing direct connections to your computer.

4. If you don't need to connect to any other computers or have them connect to you, click the Network Discovery arrow button, on the far right end, to turn off the option. The result is shown in Figure 15-6.

5. Click Start⇨Control Panel⇨Security⇨Windows Firewall⇨Change Settings and select the Block All Incoming Connections check box.

6. Connect to the network and turn on your VPN, if available.

7. When you're finished, disconnect from the VPN and the network.

8. Remember to reenable the services you want to use when you return home.

    Using public folders to send and receive files is a good option when you're on the road, but anyone on that network can see those files or folders. Be sure to keep from public locations any files that you don't want to be seen by others.

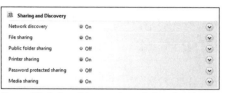

Figure 15-5: Examining your laptop's shared services

Figure 15-6: Turning off network discovery

Safely Connect Using Your Computer's Bluetooth Device

1. Click Start⊏>Control Panel⊏>Network and Internet⊏> Bluetooth Devices.

2. Click the Options tab in the window to see the dialog box shown in Figure 15-7.

3. Make sure that the Allow Bluetooth Devices to Find This Computer check box is deselected.

 Connect only to Bluetooth devices that you know the name of and can trust. Bluetooth connections establish a direct link to your computer and can be used to transmit files.

4. Click the Devices tab and select Add to connect to your device.

5. Make sure that your device is ready, and select the My Device Is Set Up and Ready to Be Found check box, shown in Figure 15-8.

6. Click Next and select the device you want to connect.

7. Click Finish to complete the process.

 If your Bluetooth device has a physical switch and you're not using it, turn it off. This action prevents unauthorized access and saves power if your laptop isn't connected to an outlet.

Figure 15-7: Bluetooth options

Figure 15-8: Adding a Bluetooth device

Getting on the Internet

Your laptop may be the engine behind your small business or just a simple appliance for your family, but chances are that the majority of your activities will revolve around some kind of connection to the Internet. The laptop can provide information, conduct business, and entertain everybody with only a few mouse clicks or keystrokes.

This chapter focuses on making your Internet browser simple and effective to use and on keeping your private information safe. You find out how to customize the look and display of your browser and how to bookmark your favorite sites and avoid sites that you don't want to see.

Chapter 16

Get ready to . . .

Set Up Your Internet Browser

1. Internet Explorer is installed in every version of Windows Vista. Click the Start button and select All Programs to see Internet Explorer listed on the program menu.

2. Click the program icon to open a browser window, as shown in Figure 16-1.

3. Choose Tools⇨Toolbars to choose commands to display at the top or side of the browser. Your choices are shown in Figure 16-2.

 Not all toolbars can be shown at the same time. You can scroll the available sidebars of Favorites, Feeds, and History through links at the top of the side toolbar.

4. Choose the Lock the Toolbars option to freeze the toolbars for future use.

 Internet Explorer is installed on Vista machines by default, but other browsers are available for your use. Popular choices include Mozilla Firefox, Apple Safari, and Opera. Each has unique advantages, so feel free to download and experiment. This book focuses on using Internet Explorer, though.

Figure 16-1: The Internet Explorer browser window

Figure 16-2: Choosing Internet Explorer toolbars

Change the Way Your Browser Views Pages

1. Open an IE browser window and click the Page button on the main toolbar.

2. From the menu shown in Figure 16-3, choose the Zoom command to change the size of pages displayed in the browser. The size is set at 100 percent by default, but you can zoom in or out, depending on your preference.

3. Choose the Text Size command to select from five text sizes, from Smallest to Largest.

 Changing the text size can affect how some Web pages are displayed, so you may want to change things back if elements on the pages you're viewing look strange.

4. To remove all toolbars and make the page fill the screen, choose Tools➪Full Screen to see the browser window in full-screen mode, as shown in Figure 16-4.

5. Move the cursor to the top of the screen to view the toolbars again and deselect the Full Screen command.

 You can press the F11 key to trigger Full Screen mode.

Figure 16-3: Zooming in a browser window

Figure 16-4: Full-screen browsing

Navigate to a Web Address

1. If you want to visit a specific Web address x, you can type it directly into the Address bar, at the top of the browser window.

 The Internet Explorer window usually ignores the omission if you leave out the www or even the http:// at the beginning of a Web address.

2. To search for a specific topic or phrase, type it in the Search bar in the upper-right corner of the browser window, as shown in Figure 16-5.

3. Click the magnifying glass icon (or press the Enter key) to begin your search. The results show up in the browser window.

4. Internet Explorer is set to search the Live Search system by default. If you would rather search by using another service (such as Google), click the down arrow at the end of the Search bar and select Find More Providers to see the Add Search Providers to Internet Explorer page, shown in Figure 16-6.

5. Click on your choices to add them to the menu. When you finish, you can access a specific search engine by clicking the down arrow next to the Search bar and choosing the one you want.

6. Click the arrow next to the Search Bar and select Change Search Defaults to change the search engine you use automatically.

7. To search text within the browser page, click the arrow and select Find On This Page. You can search for keywords or phrases from text inside the Web site you opened.

Figure 16-5: Searching the Internet

Figure 16-6: Changing your default search engine

Organize Multiple Sites with Browser Tabs

1. Open an Internet Explorer window and notice the tabs just above the sites that are displayed. The longer tab represents an open site, and a smaller tab is a link to open other tabs.

2. Click the smaller tab to open another tab in the same browser window, as shown in Figure 16-7.

 Using tabs keeps you from having multiple windows open at one time, which clutters your workspace.

3. The tab opens by default to a blank browser window. You can type another address in the Address bar now to open another site.

4. To open other tabs, click the smaller tab again.

5. Switch between tabs by clicking the tab you want. The other tabs stay open, but the focus of the browser switches to the active tab.

6. To close the tab when you're finished, click the X to the right of the tab name, as shown in Figure 16-8. The browser window itself stays open.

 Click and drag the tabs within the browser window to reorder the way they're laid out.

Figure 16-7: Opening a new Internet Explorer tab

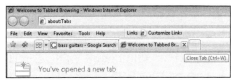

Figure 16-8: Closing a tab

Set Your Browser's Home Page

1. Open an Internet Explorer browser window and navigate to the browser window you want to open by default.

2. Click the down-arrow button to the right of the Home icon and choose Add or Change Home Page, as shown in Figure 16-9.

3. To make the site your only home page, click the Use This Webpage As Your Only Home Page radio button, shown in Figure 16-10.

4. If you want to use this page as one of a series of tabs, click the Add This Webpage to Your Home Page Tabs radio button.

 Depending on the Web pages you set as tabs in this section, your browser may take longer to open.

5. After you open all the tabs that you want to use as home tabs, click the last radio button on the list: Use the Current Tab Set As Your Home Page.

6. Click Yes to accept any changes, or click No to cancel the operation.

 Remember to put the tabs in the order you want them before making any home tab changes.

7. Click the Home icon to return to the home page or tabs at any time.

Figure 16-9: Changing your home page

Figure 10: Home page and tab choices

Bookmark Your Favorite Internet Sites

Figure 16-11: Adding a Favorite

1. Open an Internet Explorer browser window and navigate to the site you want to save.

2. Click the Add Favorites icon (the star with a plus sign on it) in the upper-left corner of the browser window and choose Add to Favorites from the drop-down menu, as shown in Figure 16-11.

3. In the Name field, type the bookmark name the way you want it to be listed, use the Create In drop-down menu to select a spot to save the bookmark, and click Add, as shown in Figure 16-12.

Figure 16-12: Favorite details

4. Click the star icon in the upper-left corner of the browser window to open the Favorites sidebar. You see your bookmark saved there.

5. Click the bookmark to return to that site at any time.

 You can drag and drop your bookmarks inside the Favorites toolbar to reorder them into whatever order you want.

 You can create folders to group similar bookmarks. Click the Add Favorites icon and select Organize Favorites to create folders and drag and drop the bookmarks into appropriate locations.

View More Information with RSS Feeds

1. Many sites use a Really Simple Syndication (RSS) feed to provide information in text form, as opposed to a full Web site. If this type of feed is available, the icon shown in Figure 16-13 is displayed in orange.

2. Click the icon to switch to RSS Feed view.

3. To subscribe to this feed, click the Add to Favorites button and select Subscribe To This Feed.

4. To view your subscriptions, click the Add Favorites icon and select the Feeds icon at the top of the Favorites sidebar, as shown in Figure 16-14.

    Subscribing to a feed allows you to have updated content delivered automatically to your browser window, as opposed to having to reload a Web page multiple times.

5. Click the specific feed link to open that feed in your browser window or tab.

    RSS feeds have multiple other uses, depending on the browser or Web sites you use and open, including downloading files and archiving feed entries.

6. Click the View Feed Properties button to change the name of the feed and specify how often the feed is updated.

Figure 16-13: The RSS icon

Figure 16-14: RSS feed subscriptions

Block Pop-Up Windows with Your Browser

1. In Internet Explorer, choose Tools⇨Pop-Up Blocker to see the current settings.

2. If the pop-up blocker is turned off, select Turn Pop-Up Blocker On.

 The Internet Explorer pop-up blocker should be enabled by default.

3. To alter the pop-up blocker settings, choose Pop-Up Blocker from the menu, as shown in Figure 16-15.

4. To allow pop-up windows from a site to open, type the Web site name in the Pop-Up Blocker Settings dialog box (see Figure 16-16) and click Add.

5. To remove a site, select it from the Allowed Sites list and click Remove.

 Allow pop-ups only from sites you absolutely trust. Pop-up windows not only are annoying but can also be used to add spyware to your computer.

6. You can alter the level of filtering of pop-up blocking from the Filter Level drop-down menu, near the bottom of the window (see Figure 16-16).

Figure 16-15: Accessing pop-up blocker settings from a menu

Figure 16-16: Allowing pop-ups from Web sites

Erase Information from Your Browser

Figure 16-17: Erasing information from your browser

1. In Internet Explorer, choose Tools⇨Delete Browsing History to open the Delete Browsing History dialog box, shown in Figure 16-17.

2. Each Web page stores a cache of files and information on the computer to speed up the browsing process. To delete these files and clear space on your computer, click the Delete Files button.

3. Click the Delete Cookies button to remove cookies from your system. (A *cookie* is a file that stores information used by Web sites to track your browsing, personal preferences, and other information.)

    Not all cookies are bad, so be careful when you're ridding your laptop of these files. You may notice differences in how your browser displays Web sites after you take this step.

4. Click Delete History to remove the list of visited Web sites from your browser.

5. Click Delete Forms to remove any trace of data related to filling out online forms.

6. On some Web sites, you can choose to save passwords for quicker access. Click Delete Passwords to remove that information.

    To clear all personal information and save a few steps, click the Delete All button at the bottom of the window.

Keep Your Browser Secure

1. Sites used for online banking or payments or other sensitive transaction information are often encrypted. Look for these two items to ensure that your transaction is secure, as shown in Figure 16-18:

   - The Web address begins with `https://` as opposed to the more standard `http://`.

   - A lock icon appears on the right end of the Address bar.

    If these items aren't present, don't use the site to transmit sensitive data. Pick up the phone or drive to your local branch instead.

2. To ensure that you're not being redirected to another site by a malicious link (a process known as *phishing*), Internet Explorer includes a phishing filter. Check its status by choosing Tools⇨Phishing Filter.

3. If the filter is turned off, select Turn On Automatic Website Checking and click the Turn On Automatic Phishing Filter radio button, as shown in Figure 16-19.

4. Check a specific Web site by choosing Tools⇨Phishing Filter⇨Check This Website. The filter ensures that the site matches its address and returns its results to you.

5. To report a possible phishing site, choose Tools⇨ Phishing Filter⇨Report This Site.

    Although this action alerts security experts to the existence of the site, your best bet is still to avoid giving information to the site and to leave the site immediately.

    Use your common sense. If a site looks wrong or something seems amiss, just leave it alone entirely.

Figure 16-18: Signs of a properly encrypted Web site

Figure 16-19: Turning on the automatic phishing filter

Part IV
Hitting the Road

Staying In Touch

Chances are that even if you have a powerful laptop, it's probably not your only computer. A laptop is the perfect complement to a desktop, allowing you to work on your projects away from the office and then move your finished files back to your main computer. If your laptop is your only computer, however, you must keep your files backed up on a separate drive to ensure that nothing happens to them. Going mobile is great, but it also makes you more susceptible to the loss of data, from accidental damage to theft.

This chapter shows you your options for backing up and syncing your data with other devices, from external hard drives to network servers to PDAs and smart phones. You can not only access your data from several different places, but also ensure that you don't lose your information even if you do somehow lose your laptop.

Get ready to . . .

Use a Virtual Briefcase

1. Right-click in a location of your choice (most likely, Documents or your desktop) and choose New➪Briefcase.

2. Drag and drop into the Briefcase the files you want to move, as shown in Figure 17-1.

    Using the Briefcase is a good way to keep files in sync over multiple computers, such as your office desktop and your laptop. You can also use it ensure that you always have backups of your important files in case of emergency.

3. Move the Briefcase to another computer or external hard drive.

4. After you make the changes you want, move the Briefcase back to your original computer and click Update This Item in the menu bar.

5. Your computer checks for differences between the original files and the Briefcase files and then presents the differences, as shown in Figure 17-2.

6. Right-click each item to determine whether to keep the original or the new copy, or if you choose to skip the sync entirely. You can also see the details of the differences between the two files to determine which action you want to take.

    The files in the Briefcase are just copies, which are linked to your originals. Don't be surprised when the files don't disappear from their original locations.

    The Briefcase shows the original location of your file and its updated status in File view, in case you have any concerns about what you're working with.

Figure 17-1: Your files in the Briefcase

Figure 17-2: Syncing your Briefcase

Use an Automatic, One-Touch Hard Drive

1. Load the external drive's software on your laptop.

2. Connect the hard drive to your computer by using a USB or FireWire connection, as shown in Figure 17-3.

3. Select the files, folders, or partitions that you want to back up using the hard drive's software.

4. Press the button on the hard drive to begin the process, as shown in Figure 17-4.

 Follow your hard drive manufacturer's directions exactly when using the one-touch backup. Failure to do so may result in losing your backup copies.

5. Set up a regular schedule for this backup.

6. To restore these backed-up files, connect the hard drive to your computer and drag and drop the files to the location you want on your laptop.

 Be sure to keep your external hard drive in a safe and secure location to ensure the safety of your backed-up data.

 Frequent backups ensure your data's safety and also make the backup process quicker because less data is being transferred each time.

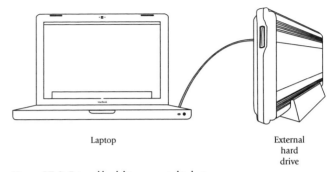

Laptop

External hard drive

Figure 17-3: External hard drive connected to laptop

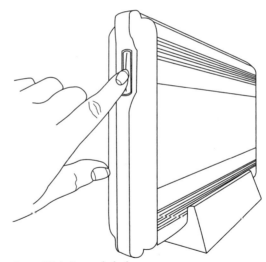

Figure 17-4: Starting the backup process

Make a Bluetooth Connection with an External Device

1. Make sure that your external device is turned on and set up to be discoverable.

2. Click Start and choose Control Panel⇨Network and Internet⇨Bluetooth Devices.

    Bluetooth can be used not only to sync mobile phones or PDAs but also to link printers, wireless keyboards, wireless mice, and other devices.

3. Click Add to see the Add Bluetooth Device Wizard dialog box, shown in Figure 17-5.

4. Select the check box and then click Next to discover the device.

5. Select the device you want to connect and select Next.

6. If necessary, enter a passkey for your device.

    If you have the option of using a passkey, use it. A passkey makes it harder for unauthorized users to access your Bluetooth connection.

7. Click Finish in the Wizard window shown in Figure 17-6 to finalize the link between your laptop and your mobile device.

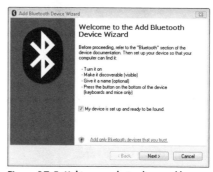

Figure 17-5: Making your device discoverable

Figure 17-6: Finalizing your Bluetooth connection

Transfer Files to a PDA or Cell Phone by Using Bluetooth

1. Connect your mobile device to your laptop by cord, wireless, or Bluetooth connection.

2. Click Start and choose All Programs➪Accessories➪ Bluetooth File Transfer Wizard.

3. As shown in Figure 17-7, specify whether you want to send a file to your device or receive a file on your laptop, and then click Next.

4. To select your device, click the Browse button (see Figure 17-8); browse for the file you want to transfer and click OK. Click Next.

5. Let the file transfer and click Finish when you're done.

6. Check your mobile device to make sure that the transfer is complete.

 This method is best used with individual files, not with mass dumps of data. Be selective in choosing information to transfer.

 Some files may not transfer, depending on your mobile device. Check with your manufacturer's instructions to be sure.

Figure 17-7: Specifying whether to send or receive files

Figure 17-8: Browsing for files to transfer

Sync Your Data to a PDA or Cell Phone

1. Install any software that came with your device on your laptop.

2. Connect your device to your laptop by way of a USB cable, wireless connection or Bluetooth.

3. Follow the directions on both the laptop and your device to sync your data.

4. Windows Mobile devices use the Sync Center, shown in Figure 17-9, to connect with your laptop. Click Start and choose Control Panel➪Network and Internet➪Sync Center to view your partnerships and check on the status of your synced data.

5. Disconnect the device from your laptop.

6. Check both your laptop and the mobile device to be sure that the data is consistent over both devices.

Figure 17-9: The Sync Center

 Most mobile devices sync contact, calendar, e-mail, and task information, whereas others may also automatically sync files or folders. Check your device's instructions for your device's full capabilities.

 If your mobile device has no information on it yet (such as when you're syncing for the first time), set your laptop to override any information coming from your mobile device. This strategy helps prevent any accidental erasure of data. Check with your device's instructions to find out how to make this happen.

Use a Flash or Hard Drive to Manually Back Up Important Documents

1. Connect your flash or external hard drive to your computer by using a USB or FireWire connection.

     Flash drives are useful for moving smaller files, whereas external hard drives may be necessary for larger files or lots of videos and songs.

2. If necessary, turn on the drive's power switch.

3. Select Open Folder to View Files from the AutoPlay window, shown in Figure 17-10. You can also click Start and select Computer to view and open your hard drive.

4. Click Start again and select Documents or Computer or another location to open a second window.

5. Drag and drop the files to the flash or external hard drive, as shown in Figure 17-11. This step makes a copy on the external drive.

6. Click on the Safely Remove Hardware icon in the lower-right corner of your desktop and select the flash or hard drive.

     Close all windows involving your flash or external hard drive before clicking the Safely Remove Hardware icon. Otherwise, you may not be able to eject the device.

7. Physically disconnect the drive from your computer.

     You maintain a lot of control over which information you back up with this method, and how often you do it, but be sure to perform these steps regularly. Otherwise, you may miss some of your data after disaster strikes.

Figure 17-10: Opening a drive from the AutoPlay window

Figure 17-11: Dragging and dropping a file

Back Up Your Information on a Server

1. Click Start and select Computer.

2. Right-click any open space in the Computer window and choose Add a Network Location from the context menu.

3. Click Next in the initial window.

4. Select the Choose a Custom Network Location option, as shown in Figure 17-12, and click Next.

5. Enter the address of your network location (see Figure 17-13) or click the Browse button to view and select available destinations and click Next.

6. Type the username for your network or leave it set to Anonymous, depending on your server's settings. Click Next.

7. Enter a name for the shortcut and click Next.

8. Click Finish to set up the shortcut.

9. Click Start⇨Computer and select the shortcut. Type the password if necessary and click OK.

10. Drag and drop the files as you would do on any other drive. Close the window when you're done.

 Check with your company's network administrator or your service provider for any server information you need in order to make this connection.

 Don't use this method on an unfamiliar or unsecure network because the information (including your password) is transferred without encryption, making it easier to steal.

 Commercial and free FTP software give you more options for transferring files, and they do it in a more secure manner than in this process. Check out the software to see whether it meets your needs.

Figure 17-12: Choosing a network connection

Figure 17-13: Entering your network address

Use the Back Up Files Wizard

1. Click Start and choose Control Panel⇨System and Maintenance⇨Backup and Restore Center.

2. Click Back Up Files.

3. Select the location you want to use, as shown in Figure 17-14. Click Next.

4. Use the check boxes to select the types of files you want to back up. This process backs up all files of this type in your profile.

5. Set the schedule for your backup, as shown in Figure 17-15, and click Save Settings and Start Backup.

6. Let the backup run until completed.

7. Make sure that the external device you're using is connected and that your computer is turned on at the scheduled backup time.

 The Back Up Files Wizard works only when the computer is turned on and connected, so be sure to stick to your schedule.

 Be sure that your device has enough space for your backups before you continue. Video and audio files can take up a great deal of space.

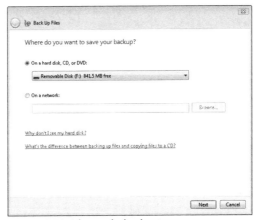

Figure 17-14: Selecting a backup location

Figure 17-15: Scheduling a backup schedule

Use the Complete Backup Wizard

1. Click Start and choose Control Panel⇨System and Maintenance⇨Backup and Restore Center (see Figure 17-16).

    This feature isn't available in Vista Home Basic or Home Premium.

2. Click Back Up Computer and select the source (either a hard drive or DVDs).

    If you're using a hard drive for this process, it must be formatted in NTFS format.

3. Click the Start Backup button in the Windows Complete PC Backup dialog box, shown in Figure 17-17.

4. Let the backup continue — it can take a long time.

5. If you're using DVDs, swap out the DVDs as required by the process.

    Make sure that you have a lot of DVDs or a large hard drive to perform this operation.

6. After the backup is complete, disconnect the media if necessary and place it in a secure location.

    This process backs up your entire computer, so you can use it in case you have to switch hard drives or recover from a serious accident. Perform the backup regularly for best results.

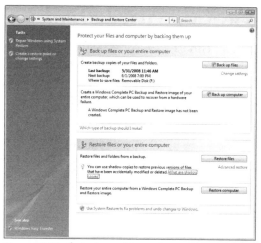

Figure 17-16: The Backup and Restore Center

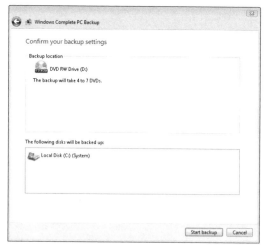

Figure 17-17: Starting your computer backup

Restore Your Complete Hard Drive

1. Reboot your computer and press F8 before the Windows logo is displayed.

2. Select Repair Your Computer in the Advanced Boot Options area and then press Enter.

3. Select your keyboard layout and click Next.

4. Select your username, enter your password, and click OK.

5. Click Windows Complete PC Restore and use the wizard to select a backup and restore your computer.

 This step erases everything on your computer and restores it from the backup. Do this task only if you have a serious problem and are positive that you want to do it.

 This task works only if you already made a backup.

Restore Individual Files from Backup

1. Click Start and choose Control Panel⇨System and Maintenance⇨Backup and Restore Center.

2. Click Restore Files and select which backup you want to restore in the Restore Files window, shown in Figure 17-18. You can select the latest backup or choose from earlier versions, depending on your needs. Click Next.

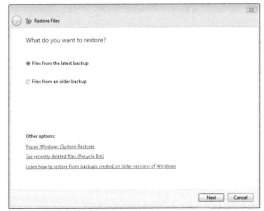

Figure 17-18: Selecting a backup location

3. Select the files and folders you want to restore, as shown in Figure 17-19. You can select any file or folder in your backup. Click Next.

4. Select the location where you want to copy the files. You can choose the file's original location or a new spot.

5. Click Start Restore to move the files back.

6. If you're moving the file back to their original location, you're asked to replace the current file, save a copy of the backup with a new name, or do nothing.

7. Delete any unnecessary files.

 This process works well only when you make regular and consistent backups. Be sure to follow your schedule religiously.

 If you have any doubts about which file to keep (the original or the backup), save both with different names. You can examine both, delete the one you don't need, and then rename to its original filename the one you kept.

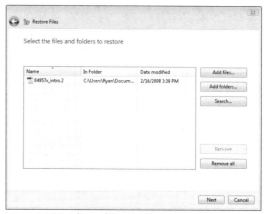

Figure 17-19: Selecting files and folders to restore

Use Windows Shadow Copy

1. Click Start and choose Control Panel⇨System and Maintenance⇨System⇨System Protection.

2. Make sure that the check box next to your hard drive is selected (see Figure 17-20) and click OK.

3. Your computer automatically creates restore points when updates are installed, or you can create a restore point manually by clicking Create.

4. To restore a file from a restore point, right-click the file and choose Restore from a Previous Version from the context menu.

5. You see available versions of the file in the Properties window, shown in Figure 17-21. Select the restore point you want to use and click Restore.

 Relying on automatic restore points is possible, but it can be an inexact science. If you're sure that you want to back something up, do it manually or use the backup function.

Figure 17-20: Enabling automatic restore points

Figure 17-21: Viewing available restore points

Playing It Safe

The situation may not be as bad as it's sometimes played up to be in news reports and other stories, but it's possible to steal data directly from your laptop. Computers and operating systems are human creations, after all — that's why the need exists for security patches, virus-protection programs, and the like. However, you can always make it harder for your computer to be hacked or your data to be stolen.

This chapter provides a few simple directions on how to better secure your laptop. Between encrypting your information and physically locking down your laptop, you can take plenty of steps to save your computer (and your mental health).

Chapter 18

Get ready to . . .

Change Your Windows Firewall Settings

1. Click Start➪Control Panel➪Security➪Windows Firewall.

2. Click Change Settings to see the Windows Firewall Settings dialog box, shown in Figure 18-1.

3. Windows Firewall should be turned on by default. If it's off, turn it on immediately.

 Never turn off Windows Firewall. Even if you're at home behind your router's firewall, Firewall provides valuable security. If you're away from your home network, it's an absolute necessity.

4. Click the Exceptions tab to see the programs that can make connections through the firewall, as shown in Figure 18-2.

5. If you're sure that a program doesn't need a firewall exception (or you no longer use that program), deselect the check box.

6. Click the Add Program button and select the program you want to make an exception for.

7. Click the Advanced tab and make sure that all your network connections (wired, wireless, and Bluetooth) are protected by the firewall.

 If a program needs to gain access through the firewall, it generally asks for it. You usually don't have to manually enable a firewall connection.

 Allow only Windows Firewall exceptions that you're absolutely sure about. If you receive a notification when you weren't expecting it, you should prevent that program from connecting.

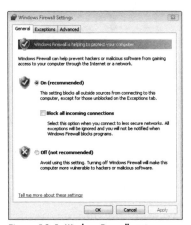

Figure 18-1: Windows Firewall settings

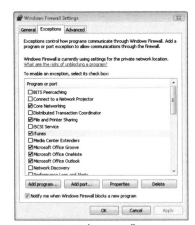

Figure 18-2: Windows Firewall exceptions

Require a Password to Use a Shared Folder

1. Click Start⇨Network⇨Network and Sharing Center.

2. Click the Password Protected Sharing arrow so that you can choose whether to turn on password-protected sharing (see Figure 18-3).

3. Click the Turn On Password Protected Sharing radio button.

 Using this feature may qualify as overkill if your computer never leaves your home network, but you should use this feature if you're heading out on the road.

4. Click Apply to finalize the setting.

5. Only someone who has accounts on your computer can access shared folders now. To add accounts, click Start⇨ Control Panel and click the Add or Remove User Accounts link, shown in Figure 18-4. More information is in Chapter 5.

 To help reduce access to your computer, be sure to delete user accounts on your computer if they're not being used.

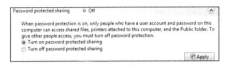

Figure 18-3: Enabling password-protected sharing

Figure 18-4: Adding and removing users

Encrypt a File or Folder

1. Navigate to the file or folder you want to encrypt.

2. Right-click the file or folder and choose Properties from the context menu. Click the Advanced button to open the Advanced Attributes dialog box, shown in Figure 18-5.

3. Select the Encrypt Contents to Secure Data check box.

4. If you're encrypting a file, click OK twice to finish the process.

5. If you're encrypting a folder, click OK twice to open the Confirm Attribute Changes dialog box, shown in Figure 18-6. Make your choice and click OK again.

6. Back up your encryption keys, as prompted from the system tray.

 Always back up your encryption keys. You may need the information later if you have to change the file settings on your laptop.

 Encrypting files and folders isn't fully supported in all versions of Vista — namely, Windows Vista Starter, Windows Vista Home Basic, and Windows Vista Home Premium.

 Encryption may slow down access to certain files and folders, but it prevents unauthorized access, even if the files or folders are removed from your computer. Encryption is a useful way to help prevent access to sensitive data.

Figure 18-5: Enabling encryption

Figure 18-6: Encrypting the contents of a folder

Set Up a Secure Password

1. When creating a secure password, use more than one word if possible, which makes it a passphrase.

2. Never use `password` or any other word that can be easily guessed.

3. Use random strings of numbers, characters, and letters if possible, as shown in Figure 18-7.

4. Use a mixture of upper- and lowercase letters, as shown in Figure 18-8.

5. The more characters you use, the harder it is to guess or hack your password.

6. Don't write your password in public areas or leave it attached to your laptop.

7. Never give your password to anybody.

 Avoid using birthdates, names of family members, or other common information that someone can easily guess.

 If you have to write down your passwords, do so in a secured area that only you have access to. Several companies make devices and programs that can help keep passwords safe and secure.

19aE74bFFg113
Figure 18-7: A random password

aBcDeFgH
Figure 18-8: A mixture of upper- and lowercase letters

Change Your Password

1. Click Start➪Control Panel➪User Accounts and Family Safety➪User Accounts.

2. Click the Change your Windows Password link to open the Change Your Password dialog box, shown in Figure 18-9.

3. Type your current password in the first text box.

4. Type your new password twice in the second and third text boxes.

5. Enter a password hint, in case you forget the password.

6. Click the Change Password button to finalize the change.

7. If you want to change the password for another account, click Start➪Control Panel➪User Accounts and Family Safety➪User Accounts➪Manage Another Account to open the Change an Account window, shown in Figure 18-10.

 Be sure that other people using your laptop know that you're changing their passwords. Not only are they prevented from accessing their accounts, but it could also cause them to lose access to their encrypted data permanently.

8. Click the Change the Password link and enter the new password and hint.

9. Click the Create Password button when you're done.

 Make sure that you remember your password. Changing it after you forget it can be difficult.

 Change your passwords periodically to keep your system secure.

Figure 18-9: Changing your password

Figure 18-10: Changing another user's password

Lock Down Your Laptop

1. Locate the lock slot on your laptop, as shown in Figure 18-11.

    This slot is a standard feature on many laptops, and you have a choice of many cables to use when you purchase one.

2. Connect the locking cable to your laptop.

3. Secure the cable around a secure, immobile anchor, as shown in Figure 18-12.

4. Lock the cable.

    This cable is especially helpful in any public area, from the coffee shop to your office desk. Use it wherever you feel necessary (and some places where you feel it isn't).

5. Leave the laptop locked until you're ready to move on.

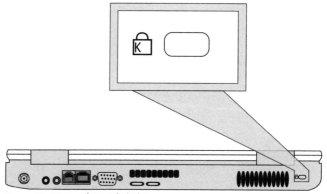

Figure 18-11: Your laptop's lock slot

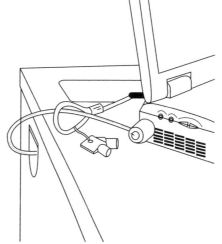

Figure 18-12: Latching your laptop to an immobile surface

Part V
What Could Go Wrong?

The 5th Wave   By Rich Tennant

"They won't let me through security until I remove the bullets from my Word document."

Troubleshooting Your Hardware

As advanced as your laptop is, it's still made of moving parts. Add to that the movement and bumps that your computer can endure, and something is bound to fail at some point. The first step in maintaining your laptop should be to purchase a multiyear warranty and know exactly which problems are covered. Your laptop (and the data contained within it) is valuable enough to protect with a decent plan. Think of it as car insurance for your laptop.

It's especially important to have a plan because you can replace few parts on a laptop. Unlike on a desktop tower, everything in a laptop has been shrunk and arranged to provide the maximum amount of power in a minimum amount of space. For this reason, some form of technical training is necessary to replace hardware. Still, there are a few things you can do to find the problem and determine whether you should purchase only new parts or just buy a new laptop. This chapter walks you through those steps.

Chapter 19

Get ready to . . .

Find Out Why the Screen Is Black

1. Make sure your laptop is powered on.

2. If you're sure that it is, find out whether you can see text when the computer first starts up. If you can, the screen is okay and the problem lies with your operating system.

3. If you see no text or images on the screen at any time, connect your laptop to an external monitor.

4. If you can see part of your desktop on the external monitor, right-click the desktop and choose Personalize⇨ Display Settings to open the Display Settings dialog box, shown in Figure 19-1.

5. See whether your laptop's monitor is listed under these settings.

6. When you see your display on an external monitor, it means that your screen is malfunctioning. All your data is safe, and your computer is still functional — you just need a new laptop monitor.

7. If you don't see a display on either monitor, it means that your video card is bad. Depending on how your laptop is built, you may have to replace the motherboard.

Figure 19-1: Display settings

 For a short-term solution, you can use your laptop connected to an external monitor. Make the external monitor your main display in the Display Settings dialog box and work normally.

 You can't replace any of monitor parts yourself. Take the monitor to a qualified repairperson or return it to the manufacturer for maintenance.

Find Out Why Lines Appear on the Screen

1. Make sure that the line or lines are the result of a monitor malfunction and not a part of a software malfunction. If the line extends over multiple windows or the toolbar at the bottom of your screen (unlike in the screen shown in Figure 19-2), the lines are part of the monitor and not the software.

2. Move the monitor around. If the lines come and go, the problem might be a loose connection between the monitor and the motherboard.

3. If the lines stay on your monitor, plug in an external monitor and set it to mirror your desktop.

4. If the external monitor looks normal, the problem lies in your laptop's monitor.

5. If the external monitor shows the same flaw, the problem lies in your video card.

 Again, none of these parts is easily replaceable. Let a qualified professional help you.

 More than likely, this problem won't damage your files. Regardless, you should always perform a backup before your computer is worked on.

Figure 19-2: A screen line not caused by a hardware malfunction

Find Out Why Your Keyboard Is Typing Incorrectly or Not Working

1. Open Microsoft Word, Notepad, or another text program and type a short phrase.

2. If certain keys aren't working, make a note of which ones are malfunctioning and use a can of compressed air to blow any debris out of the laptop.

3. If typing produces unusual characters, click Start⇨ Control Panel and choose Change Keyboards or Other Input Methods under the Clock, Language and Region Settings Header to see the Regional and Language Options dialog box, shown in Figure 19-3.

4. Click the Change Keyboards button and make sure that your keyboard is set to the correct language.

5. If the correct language is selected, click Start⇨Control Panel⇨Ease of Access⇨Change How Your Keyboard Works and deselect the options to turn on mouse keys, filter keys, and sticky keys, as shown in Figure 19-4.

6. If none of these steps works, or if your keyboard isn't responding, plug in an external keyboard and see whether you have the same problems using it. If the external keyboard works, the problem lies with your laptop keyboard.

 You may find Mouse Keys, Filter Keys, and Sticky Keys useful, but turn them on only if you know what they do and why you want to use them.

 Using an external keyboard, you can still use your laptop, and your data is more than likely safe. Although this problem should be fairly simple to fix on most laptops, make a backup before any repairs are performed.

Figure 19-3: Checking your keyboard language

Figure 19-4: Disabling keyboard settings

Find Out Why Your Mouse Is Moving Strangely or Not Working

1. Plug in an external mouse and see whether it behaves the same as your track pad or pointer stick.

2. If the external mouse works well, the problem lies with your laptop's hardware.

3. If the external mouse behaves the same way, click Start⇨ Control Panel and select Mouse under the Hardware and Sound heading.

4. In the Mouse Properties dialog box, shown in Figure 19-5, ensure that the ClickLock and Switch Primary and Secondary Buttons features are disabled. Skim the options on the other tabs to ensure that the settings are correct there too.

5. If Step 4 doesn't solve the problem, click Start⇨Control Panel⇨Ease of Access⇨Change How My Mouse Works and make sure that the Turn On Mouse Keys check box is selected, as shown in Figure 19-6.

6. If none of these steps works, the problem lies in your laptop's hardware. Take it to a qualified repairperson.

 Depending on how you feel about your laptop's track pad or pointer stick, you may prefer to use an external mouse. If the laptop repair cost is a factor, an external mouse is a suitable option.

 None of these parts can be easily replaced — contact the manufacturer or a qualified repairperson.

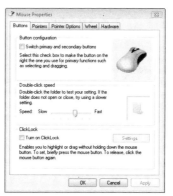

Figure 19-5: Mouse settings

Figure 19-6: Turning off mouse keys

Find Out Why Your Computer Doesn't Start

1. Connect the power supply to your laptop, if you haven't already.

2. If your laptop starts up now, your battery is probably loose or discharged. Make sure that it's inserted correctly and that the charge indicator light is showing power. If your battery is charged and it still doesn't work, the problem lies either with the battery connections or the battery itself.

3. If your laptop doesn't start now, examine what happens. If it starts to boot up and then stalls, the problem could be caused by the software.

4. If you hear a loud clicking noise and the startup process stalls, you might have a hard drive problem.

5. If your laptop doesn't start up, the problem could be caused by anything from the power button to the memory to the motherboard. Take the laptop to your repairperson.

6. If you see the "blue screen of death" (see Figure 19-7), the problem could be a malfunctioning piece of hardware or software. Try removing any hardware you just installed or starting your computer while holding down the F8 key to enter Safe mode.

7. If your laptop can start up in Safe mode, try uninstalling any newly installed software by clicking Start➪Control Panel➪Uninstall a Program and restarting your computer.

8. If none of these steps works, take your laptop to a qualified repairperson.

 These steps illustrate why you should make backups of your data: When you take your laptop in for repair, be sure to ask for backup copies of your data, if possible.

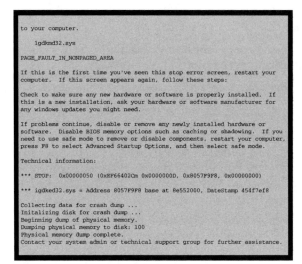

Figure 19-7: The blue screen of death

Find Out Why Your Can't Connect a Device to Your Computer

1. Make sure that you've loaded all the correct software for your device.

2. If your device requires external power, make sure that it's connected and turned on.

3. Click the Start button, right-click Computer, and choose Manage.

4. Select Device Manager (as shown in Figure 19-8) and see whether your device is listed.

5. If your device is listed, try disconnecting other USB devices to see whether they're interfering with this device.

6. If your laptop doesn't recognize the device, try using another USB or FireWire cable, if possible.

7. Try connecting your device to another computer. If it works, the problem lies with your laptop. If it doesn't work, it's probably the device itself.

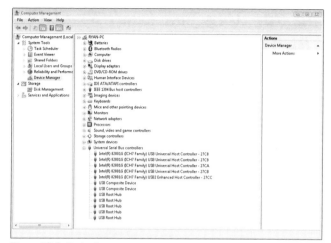

Figure 19-8: Device Manager

 Unless you're trying to connect an external drive, your laptop probably isn't in danger of losing any data. Just be sure to make a backup before making any repairs.

 Use external power supplies whenever possible. Your laptop can power only so many devices before it just doesn't have any power left.

 If you're using a hub with multiple USB connections, try taking it out and connecting the device directly before blaming the device or laptop itself.

Find Out Why You Can't Read CDs or DVDs

1. Examine the disc and make sure that no fingerprints, scratches, or debris are on the disc.

2. Make sure that you inserted the disc in the drive correctly. (Don't laugh — an upside-down disc may seem foolish, but it's an easy problem to fix.)

3. If your optical drive can be removed, remove it and reseat it to make sure that it's connected properly.

4. Make sure that you can see the disc under Start⇨ Computer, as shown in Figure 19-9.

5. If you can't see the disc, try inserting another one. If the second disc works, the problem is with the first disc.

6. If your drive doesn't read any disc you give it, the problem is with your drive.

Figure 19-9: An available DVD

 A "bad" disc might still be readable on another computer. Depending how the disc was burned, another drive might be able to read it. Always try using the disc on another system.

 Some laptops have modular drives, which means that you can remove a bad one and insert a good one.

 If you don't have a modular drive, have a qualified repairperson look at it. The problem could be the drive or the motherboard.

Troubleshooting Your Software

Chapter

20

Most of the time, the software you install on your computer runs with no problem. Vista itself and other programs you add have been designed to operate in the same space without interfering with each other. However, you may occasionally run into problems with programs. For example, installing a Vista update may cause problems with older programs, a file may become corrupt and sabotage a program, or an outdated driver might prevent your computer from booting up.

When something goes wrong, you want to get it fixed as soon as you can. This chapter helps you deal with these occurrences and gets your computer up and running with as quickly and easily as possible.

Get ready to . . .

Start Your Computer in Safe Mode

1. If your computer doesn't boot up correctly, restart it by holding down the power button until the computer shuts down, wait a minute, and then press it again.

2. Before you see the Windows logo or the progress bar at the bottom of the screen, press and hold the F8 key, shown in Figure 20-1.

3. From the menu that appears, select Last Known Good Configuration to see whether your computer begins running normally.

4. If Step 3 fails, repeat Steps 1 and 2.

5. Select Safe Mode. Log in to your computer, if possible.

 This step is usually necessary only when an update or program you installed is causing problems with the computer's startup operation. Use Safe mode to remove any programs you recently installed to see whether the problem is fixed.

6. Use Safe mode to explore your system and remove files or programs that may be causing a problem.

Reinstall Your Operating System

1. Insert your laptop's Restore disc (available from the manufacturer) or your Windows Vista disc.

2. Restart your computer and allow it to boot from the CD or DVD.

3. Follow the instructions from there to reinstall the operating system.

 You may see the boot selection screen if you improperly shut down your computer. In this case, select Start Windows Normally to see whether your computer starts properly.

 This lesson makes your laptop's operating system function again, but it means that you're starting from scratch. All your files and programs will be erased, unless you backed them up elsewhere. Follow this step *only* as a last resort.

F8

Figure 20-1: The F8 key

 To avoid accidentally erasing your information, be sure to disconnect any external hard drives or flash drives before reinstalling your operating system.

Uninstall Problem Software

1. Click Start and choose Control Panel⇨Software⇨ Uninstall a Program.

2. In the list displayed in the Programs and Features window, shown in Figure 20-2, click the software you want to remove and click the Uninstall button that appears at the top of the window.

3. Confirm your decision and click Yes or No, as shown in Figure 20-3.

4. You're notified when this operation is complete.

5. Repeat this process as necessary by clicking additional programs and uninstalling them.

 You can also use this process to remove software you no longer want to use or to clear space on your computer.

 Not all software uninstalls in the same way. Be sure to check the folders in C:\Program Files to see whether all files were removed.

 Always uninstall software before deleting information in C:\ Program Folders. Completing this task before uninstalling software can cause problems down the road.

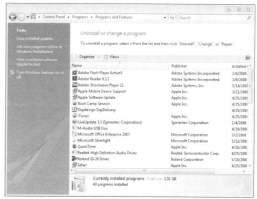

Figure 20-2: Uninstalling software

Figure 20-3: Confirming your decision

Repair and Reinstall Malfunctioning Software

1. Click Start and choose Control Panel⇨Software⇨ Uninstall a Program.

2. Click to select the program that's causing a problem on the list, and look at the toolbar shown in Figure 20-4.

3. Depending on the software you selected, you may see options to change or repair the software.

4. Click the Change button to modify the installation of the program, such as adding or removing features.

5. Click the Repair button, if it's available (see Figure 20-5) to reinstall files and make the program functional again.

 Use this option if you want to keep the program but it's causing problems. A reinstallation should restore the program to its normal functioning status.

6. Run through the instructions and click Finish to end the process, if applicable.

7. Try using the program again. If it still doesn't work, uninstall the program and reinstall it from your original disc or download.

 Repair and Change options differ depending on the program. Refer to the software instructions and the available options for more information.

 Back up any files associated with the program you select before you uninstall it, just to be sure that you have everything you might need. The uninstall process removes settings and templates you might want to save. You also have to reinstall any patches or updates if you put the program back on your laptop.

Figure 20-4: The Uninstall, Change, and Repair buttons

Figure 20-5: The QuickTime Repair or Remove dialog box

Uninstall Problem Hardware Drivers

1. Click Start and right-click the Computer option.

2. Choose Manage from the pop-up menu.

3. Click Device Manager in the Computer Management window to display the list shown in Figure 20-6.

4. Right-click the name of the device that's causing problems and choose Uninstall.

5. Confirm the uninstall process, as shown in Figure 20-7.

6. Download a driver from the device manufacturer, or get one from the device's installation disc.

 Make sure that you have updated drivers to reinstall before beginning this process.

7. Reinstall the driver to reactivate the device.

 Most of your laptop's main components are already contained in the computer, so you should already have the right drivers from your manufacturer. Follow this step for additional hardware or corrupted drivers.

 You can also use this process to uninstall drivers for devices you don't use any more, if a device still shows up in the Device Manager list. Remember, though, that your laptop always tries to reinstall devices contained internally.

Figure 20-6: Device Manager

Figure 20-7: Confirming the uninstall process

Update Hardware Drivers

1. Click Start and right-click the Computer option.

2. Choose Manage from the pop-up menu.

3. Click Device Manager in the Computer Management window.

4. Right-click the device you want to update and choose Update Driver Software.

5. In the dialog box shown in Figure 20-8, select whether you want to search automatically or select a specific location.

6. If you choose the automatic selection, your laptop checks online (if you have a network connection) and searches your machine for updates, as shown in Figure 20-9.

 Because searches are time-consuming and sometimes inefficient, having a specific location from which to install a new driver is a quicker strategy.

7. If you downloaded a new driver, click the Browse My Computer for Driver Software link, navigate to the location where you saved the driver, and then select the new driver. You may have to extract the driver from a .zip file.

8. Follow the driver's directions and click Finish to finalize the installation.

 This lesson works best when you download new or updated drivers from the manufacturer's Web site or when they're delivered as part of an update.

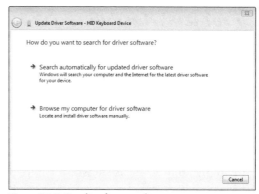

Figure 20-8: Searching for a new driver

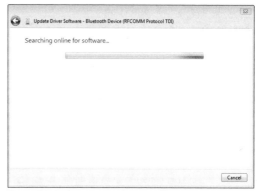

Figure 20-9: The automatic driver installation

Patching It Up

*Y*our laptop may have come fully loaded with software, or maybe your IT professional or spouse (maybe they're one and the same) set up your computer for you. Even considering that level of care, changes need to be made. Software never works perfectly, and something else always needs to be tweaked, added, or removed.

Everything from your individually loaded software to Vista itself needs patching, and most programs have the functionality to look for those changes by themselves. Seeking out these patches yourself is a good idea — the patches can improve the functionality of your laptop and keep it secure from viruses and hacking threats. From improving program performance to closing security holes, patching your laptop software is an important and necessary step in using your laptop.

Chapter

21

Get ready to . . .

Automatically Patch Your Operating System

1. Click Start➪All Programs➪Internet Explorer or click the Internet Explorer shortcut on the Quick Launch bar, if your laptop has one.

2. In Internet Explorer, click the Tools button and choose Windows Update, as shown in Figure 21-1.

3. Windows Update displays your system's patch status and announces whether any important updates are available, as shown in Figure 21-2.

4. Click the View Available Updates link and click Install.

5. Windows Update downloads and installs the updates you chose. You may have to restart your system after the process is complete. Repeat this process until no more critical patches are available.

 There's no way around it: Your computer must be connected to the Internet in order to use Windows Update.

 Applying patches to your operating system occasionally causes problems with your software. It doesn't happen often, but a little research can be helpful. Check the software manufacturer's Web site if you're concerned or have had problems in the past.

 When a patch is listed as critical, the security of your system is at stake. You can pass up optional patches, if you want, but you should always install critical patches when they're listed and available.

 You may notice large update packages called Service Packs. These major update collections should be installed after you do your research to see how they're affecting other computers and their functions.

Figure 21-1: Finding the Windows Update link

 Windows Update can also check for updates to Microsoft Office products and some device drivers as well as operating system patches.

 Windows Update is also available by clicking Start➪All Programs➪ Windows Update.

Figure 21-2: Your computer's patching status

Add Individual Patches to Your Operating System

1. Click Start⇨All Programs⇨Windows Update.

2. Click Check for Updates to display the Windows Update window, shown in Figure 21-3.

3. After the search is done, click View Available Updates to see all updates, both critical and optional.

4. Select the check boxes for any updates you want to install, as shown in Figure 21-4.

5. Click Install to add the patch to your system.

 Optional patches can range from language packs to optional software programs and other add-ins. It's up to you to balance the need for these patches against the time and effort involved and the amount of disk space the patches will occupy. Remember that your laptop will run fine without them.

 If you no longer want to see optional updates in your list, highlight the ones you want to delete, right-click them, and choose Hide Updates. To see the updates again, click the Restore Hidden Updates link (refer to Figure 21-2).

Figure 21-3: Viewing available updates

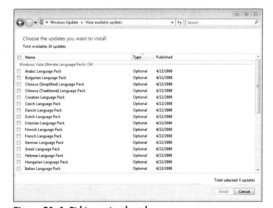

Figure 21-4: Picking optional patches

Find Patches for Other Pieces of Software

1. Click Start➪All Programs➪Internet Explorer.

2. Navigate to the software manufacturer's Web site and look for the Support section or Downloads section, as shown in Figure 21-5.

3. Search for the product you own and find its page, as shown in Figure 21-6.

4. Download and install the patch (if any) that you find on the site to update your software.

 The layout obviously changes from Web site to Web site, but this process works for the vast majority of software manufacturers.

 Before installing a software patch, search the Internet to research how the patch will affect your laptop. Patches are tested before being released, but a little real-world experience is usually helpful.

 Check for notices on manufacturer Web sites and technical news sites to see when new patches are available and why you should install them.

Figure 21-5: A Web site's Support section

Figure 21-6: Downloading updated software

Allow Your Software to Find Its Own Patches

1. Open the program you want to check and look for the Updates command, usually in the Help section of the menu bar. An example is shown in Figure 21-7.

2. Click the Check For Updates (or something similar) command to make the program contact its manufacturer.

3. If the program is up-to-date, you see a message like the one shown in Figure 21-8.

4. If any updates are available, install the patch.

5. Depending on how often you check for updates, you may have to repeat steps 2 through 4 and restart your computer to ensure that everything is installed.

 Some manufacturers include automatic update programs in their installations. Let the update programs run when necessary to update any applicable programs.

 This list of steps gives you a general outline for updating your laptop's software. The process may not work exactly this way, but you should be able to find similar steps in most programs.

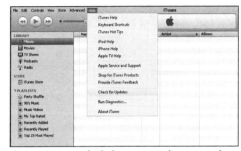

Figure 21-7: An individual program's Update command

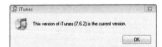

Figure 12-8: An update notification

Automate Your Update Schedule

1. Click Start⇨All Programs⇨Windows Update.

2. Click the Change Settings link, shown in Figure 21-9.

3. Use the drop-down menus in the Change Settings dialog box to specify the time and date on which you want your computer to check with Windows Update (see Figure 21-10).

4. Specify whether you want the updates to install automatically, download only, or simply notify you of the availability of patches.

5. Click OK to finalize your settings.

Figure 21-9: Changing your update settings

 Your computer must be turned on and connected to the Internet to run automatic updates.

 You don't have to check for updates every day — once a week is usually enough. Microsoft usually releases patches on Tuesdays.

 Pay attention to technical news reports in case a special patch is necessary and ready to install.

Figure 21-10: Setting your update schedule

Set Up Your Own Update Schedule

1. Make a list of the software on your computer and note where patches are available.

2. Use a calendar or scheduling assistant (such as Windows Calendar — click Start⇨All Programs⇨Windows Calendar) to set up regular reminders.

3. Follow the reminders to install patches and updates.

Part VI
Options

The 5th Wave   By Rich Tennant

"This program's really helped me learn a new language. It's so buggy I'm constantly talking with overseas service reps."

Your Instant Office

Whether you work for a huge multinational corporation or your own home business, most people use their laptops for business purposes. The mobility and functionality of the laptop make it a wonderful tool for conducting business in your office or on the road. Wherever you go, you have access to your important files and information, and you can show off your information wherever you are.

This chapter shows you how to use your office tools at home or away from home. It also focuses on software included with Vista and Microsoft Office 2007, which must be purchased separately. Outlook 2007 is geared more toward corporate users, whereas Windows Mail, Calendar, and Contacts handle the needs of smaller users. No matter which version you have, though, you should be able to follow these tasks and get your needs met with a minimum of effort.

Chapter 22

Get ready to . . .

Add Events to Windows Calendar

1. Click Start➪All Programs➪Windows Calendar.

2. In the Calendar window shown in Figure 22-1, click the calendar in the upper-left corner to navigate to the date you want.

3. Enter the name and location of an appointment, along with its start and end times, on the right side of the window (see Figure 22-2).

   You can use different colors to differentiate between appointment types or priorities. Select a color in each appointment window to start your own color-coding system.

4. If you want a reminder, click the drop-down arrow in the Reminder section and specify how long before the event you want to be reminded.

5. If you want the appointment to recur every day, week, month, or year, select that option from the Recurrence drop-down menu.

6. Your appointment is automatically saved.

7. To see different views of your calendar, click the View button at the top and select Day, Week, Work Week, or Month.

8. To delete an event, right-click it and click the Delete button.

   A calendar works well only when you check and update it regularly. To get the most benefit from your calendar, make checking it a part of your daily routine.

Figure 22-1: Navigating your calendar

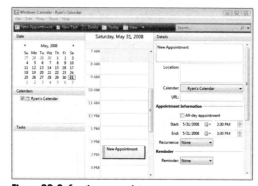

Figure 22-2: Creating an appointment

Create Multiple Windows Calendars

1. Click Start⇨All Programs⇨Windows Calendar.

2. Click File⇨New Calendar to see the new calendar, shown in Figure 22-3.

3. Give the new calendar a name to differentiate it from the original calendar.

4. Select a new color for the calendar — appointments from different calendars show up on the same schedule in different colors.

5. Keep both calendars selected to view all appointments, as shown in Figure 22-4.

6. To see only specific appointments, select the check boxes for only the calendars you want to view.

 This is a good strategy if you want to keep your business and personal schedules separate, but you should still keep track of all of them in one place.

 Create as many calendars as you need to keep tracks of multiple types of events — let your schedule determine the best way to track it.

Figure 22-3: Creating a calendar

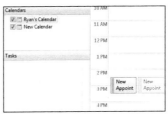

Figure 22-4: Viewing all calendar events

Publish and Share Your Windows Calendar

1. Click Start➪All Programs➪Windows Calendar.

2. Select the check boxes for the calendars you want to publish.

3. Click Share on the menu bar and choose Publish from the menu to view the Publish Calendar dialog box, shown in Figure 22-5.

4. Enter the name of your calendar and select the check boxes for the types of information you want to include.

5. Click Browse to navigate to the location for your published calendar. You can either choose a network location (such as a shared folder) or a place on your computer.

6. Click Publish to export your calendar. You can also select the Automatically Publish Changes Made to This Calendar check box to republish your calendar each time you make changes.

7. To subscribe to a calendar, click Share➪Subscribe and navigate to the calendar's location (see Figure 22-6).

8. To send your calendar by e-mail, click Share➪Send via E-mail. You must have a Windows Mail account set up to use this function.

 Make sure that the location for your published calendar is accessible to everyone you want to see it. A good place might be a public folder in your account or a shared folder on your network.

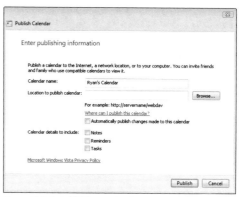

Figure 22-5: Publishing a calendar

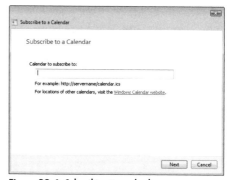

Figure 22-6: Subscribing to a calendar

Add People to Windows Contacts

1. Click Start and choose All Programs➪Windows Contacts.

2. From the menu bar (see Figure 22-7), click New Contact.

   You can also use contact information from Windows Contacts in Windows Calendar and Windows Mail, making it an especially valuable tool.

3. In the Properties dialog box, shown in Figure 22-8, enter all the information you know.

   Enter as much information as possible in the Contact record — more information makes the record more useful later.

4. Click the tabs to enter more information, such as addresses and notes.

5. Click the picture to add a photo to your laptop or remove it from that contact record.

6. Click OK to save the contact.

7. If someone gives you an electronic business card, such as a file with the .vcf extension, click Import from the menu bar shown in Figure 22-7, choose that file type, and navigate to the location of the file.

8. Select the file and click OK twice to add it to your contacts list.

   Keep your contacts as up-to-date as possible. It's frustrating to try to use an old e-mail address or disconnected phone number to contact someone.

Figure 22-7: The Contacts window

Figure 22-8: Adding contact information

Communicate with Windows Messenger

1. Click Start and choose All Programs⇨Windows Live Messenger Download, if you haven't already downloaded it. Follow the instructions to install Windows Live Messenger.

2. If you have a Hotmail or MSN account, use that e-mail address and password. Otherwise, sign up for an account using the Sign Up for a Windows Live ID link near the bottom of the dialog box shown in Figure 22-9.

3. Sign in using your username and password. Select the appropriate check boxes if you want to save your username and password and if you want to sign in automatically when you log in to your computer.

4. After you log in, the window shown in Figure 22-10 opens. Any contacts you associated with your e-mail account are listed in the Messenger list.

5. Click the plus icon on the side of the Find a Contact field to add contacts to your list. You need to use the e-mail address associated with the person's Windows Messenger account.

6. After you add contacts to your list, you can see whether they're signed in. To initiate a chat, double-click you're a friend's icon and send a message.

7. Windows Messenger stays open even if you close all the windows. To exit, right-click the icon in the notification area and choose Exit.

 You can also use Windows Messenger to send messages to mobile devices.

Figure 22-9: The Windows Messenger sign-in window

Figure 22-10: The Windows Messenger main window

 In addition to sending messages, you can send files and pictures by way of Windows Messenger.

Set Up Outlook E-Mail

1. Click Start and choose All Programs⇨Microsoft Office⇨ Microsoft Office Outlook 2007.

2. If this is your first time using Outlook, click Next twice at startup to enable an e-mail account. Otherwise, click Tools⇨E-mail Accounts and choose Add a New E-Mail Account.

3. To set up your account manually, select the Manually Configure Server Settings check box in the Auto Account Setup dialog box and then click Next, as shown in Figure 22-11. This step is usually the quickest because you can specifically choose your e-mail settings.

 Every service provider or company has its own, individual e-mail server settings, so you must get your account information from someone there before setting up your e-mail account.

4. Choose Internet e-mail or Exchange e-mail, depending on your account settings, and then click Next.

5. Enter your information in the Add New E-Mail Account dialog box, shown in Figure 22-12 and click the Test Account Settings button to make sure that your mail works correctly.

6. After you test the settings, click Next and then Finish to add the account.

 You can have several different e-mail accounts coming into Outlook, such as a work account, a personal account, and a junk mail account. Add as many as you need.

Figure 22-11: Manually configuring your e-mail

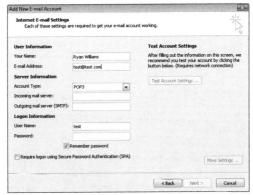

Figure 22-12: E-mail account settings

Add Outlook Calendar Events

1. Click Start and choose All Programs⇨Microsoft Office⇨ Microsoft Office Outlook 2007.

2. Select Calendar in the left column to see Calendar view, shown in Figure 22-13.

3. Click the New button in the upper-left corner to create an appointment, as shown in Figure 22-14.

4. Enter the time, date, subject, and location information.

5. Click the lock icon to make the appointment private and inaccessible to other people looking at your calendar.

6. Click the 15 Minutes drop-down arrow in the Options group to set reminder times.

 You see reminders for appointments only if Outlook 2007 is open. Otherwise, you can't use those functions.

7. Click Recurrence to set up a repeating appointment.

8. Click the Save & Close button to put the appointment on your calendar.

 Outlook 2007 has the same calendar functions as Windows Calendar but can also schedule meetings for multiple attendees, handle several different calendars based on a server, and perform many other functions. Check with your company's network administrator for more information on how to use them.

Figure 22-13: Outlook Calendar view

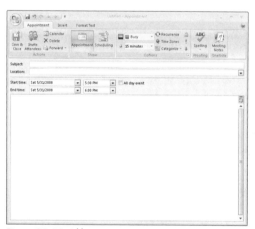

Figure 22-14: Adding an appointment

Add Outlook Contacts

1. Click Start and choose All Programs⇨Microsoft Office⇨Microsoft Office Outlook 2007.

2. Click Contacts to see your available contacts.

3. Click the New button on the toolbar in the upper-left corner to add a contact.

4. On the contact record shown in Figure 22-15, enter as much information as possible.

     You can store multiple e-mail addresses, phone numbers, and mailing addresses for each contact. Click the arrow on the drop-down menus next to each field for more information.

5. Click the Save & Close button when you finish.

6. To access your contact information, double-click the record. A virtual card opens, showing all the information you have on that contact.

     You can also click the E-Mail, Meeting, or Call buttons in the Communicate group to initiate contact from that record.

     Contact records are automatically accessible to Microsoft Outlook 2007 e-mail accounts. When sending a new message, click the To button in the e-mail message to add a contact's e-mail address.

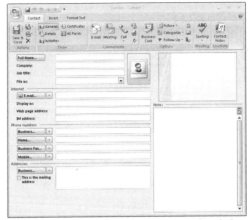

Figure 22-15: An empty contact record in Microsoft Outlook 2007

Add Outlook Tasks

1. Click Start and choose All Programs⇨Microsoft Office⇨ Microsoft Office Outlook 2007.

2. Click the Tasks button in the left column.

3. Select the New button in the upper-left corner to see the reminder page shown in Figure 22-16.

4. Enter the task's subject name, start and due dates, status, priority, and percentage-completed information.

5. Add notes in the field at the bottom of the record.

6. Select the Reminder check box to set a reminder to occur before the due date of the task.

7. Click the Save & Close button to add the task to your list.

Figure 22-16: Adding a task

 A task list is a good way to centralize all your to-do lists and then accurately track them. The more often you update the list, the better it works.

 If you're using an Exchange system, you can assign the task to somebody else or send a status report using the toolbar at the top of the task.

Use Office Templates

1. Click Start and select All Programs⇨Microsoft Office.

2. Open the Office application of your choice — in this example, I use Word.

3. Click the Office Start button in the upper-left corner of Word and select New.

4. In the Templates (left) column of the New window, shown in Figure 22-17, select the category for the template you want to use.

5. Scroll through the choices until you find the exact template you want. In this case, I'm looking at a letter accepting a job offer.

 Many templates are available for each Office application, depending on what you need. All are available by clicking the New button in whichever application you're using.

6. As shown in Figure 22-18, the template creates a basic outline of the document with fields in which to enter your information. Modify and save the document however you want.

 Templates are designed to be modified and changed according to your own needs and specifications. Don't be afraid to use templates as a starting point and move elements around from there.

Figure 22-17: Choosing a Microsoft Office template

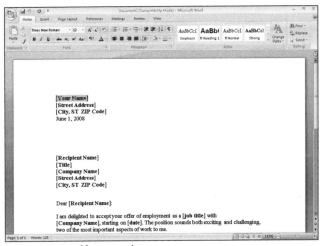

Figure 22-18: Modifying a template

Connect Your Laptop to a Docking Station

1. Set up your docking station and connect any peripheral devices you have, such as an external monitor, a keyboard, and a mouse.

    The docking station is an easy way to create a desktop-like environment in your office without having to buy another computer. You can also use a full-size keyboard, mouse, and monitor, if you prefer.

2. Connect your laptop to the docking station (see Figure 22-19).

3. Start the laptop and log in to Windows as usual.

4. Use the external peripherals as you would use them on a normal computer.

5. To disconnect the laptop from the docking station, click Start and select the arrow next to the power option. Choose to either shut down the laptop or eject it from the docking station.

6. Manually disconnect the laptop from the docking station.

    Always be sure that your computer is either powered off or prepared for disconnection before removing your laptop. Failure to do so could harm the laptop, the docking station, or both.

    Not all laptops have docking stations created for them — check the manufacturer's information to see what's available. Otherwise, you can still place external peripherals in a single area and plug them all into your laptop manually.

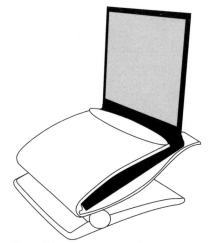

Figure 22-19: Connecting your laptop to a docking station

Connect Your Laptop to a Projector

1. Click Start and choose Control Panel⇨Mobile PC⇨ Adjust Settings Before Giving a Presentation.

2. As shown in Figure 22-20, create your presentation settings and click OK.

3. Under Mobile PC, click Windows Mobility Center.

4. In the Windows Mobility Center, shown in Figure 22-21, click the Turn On button in the Presentation Settings section.

5. Connect your laptop to the projector by using a VGA or DVI connection.

6. Power on the projector.

7. In the Windows Mobility Center, click the Connect Display button to make the laptop detect the projector.

8. Use the laptop as you normally do, with your desktop appearing in sync with the projector.

 Some laptops may have function key sequences that send video signals from laptops to projectors. Check the manufacturer's information.

 Complete all of your connections and settings before turning on the projector. Not only do you avoid exposing any information you don't want anybody else to see, but you also save wear and tear on the expensive projector bulbs.

Figure 22-20: Creating presentation settings

Figure 22-21: Turning on projector settings

Share Files in Windows Live Messenger

1. Start Windows Live Messenger and sign in to your account.

2. Click the Sharing Folder icon (it's second from the left on the Messenger toolbar) to see the Sharing Folders window, shown in Figure 22-22.

3. Click the Share a Folder with a Contact link to choose the contact you want to share with, as shown in Figure 22-23.

4. Click the folder created in that user's name and select OK to open.

5. Click Add Files or drag files into the folder to put items in your sharing folder for your contact to retrieve.

 Large files may take a long time to share and download, depending on the speed of your Internet connections.

6. Your contact can now retrieve files from that folder.

 Both you and your contact must be online to share items.

Figure 22-22: Sharing folders in Windows Live Messenger

Figure 22-23: Choosing a contact in Sharing Folders

Change Your Status and Personal Message in Windows Live Messenger

1. Start Windows Live Messenger and sign in to your account.

2. Click the drop-down menu next to your name in the Windows Live Messenger window.

3. Select the status you want (see Figure 22-24), and it changes immediately. Depending on your status message, contacts see different notices when they try to contact you.

 If you change your status to Appear Offline, nobody can contact you by way of Live Messenger. This applies to all contacts.

4. To change your personal message, click the line below your account name, as shown in Figure 22-25.

5. Type the personal message you want to use.

 Remember that your personal message is visible to all contacts, professional or personal. Consider this fact when you type a personal message.

6. Press Return to finish typing and display your message.

Figure 22-24: Changing your status

Figure 22-25: Changing your personal message

Mainstream Media

*M*ost installations of Windows Vista come with all the entertainment options you need. Between Windows Media Player (which handles the vast majority of audio and video files as well as DVDs) and any other free media programs available for download, all the basic entertainment functions are covered. However, two versions of Vista, both of which are available for laptops, come with the souped-up program Windows Media Center. Think of it as a portable home-entertainment center.

This chapter takes a quick look at Windows Media Center and helps you understand the program better. You find out how to make it work and how to customize it to your needs. With Windows Media Center on your computer, you get more than the basics — you get the full experience.

Chapter

23

Get ready to . . .

Navigate Windows Media Center

1. Click Start⇨All Programs⇨Windows Media Center.

2. After Windows Media Center opens, move the mouse cursor to view the controls shown in Figure 23-1.

3. Click the green Start button in the upper-left corner to return to the main Windows Media Center screen from wherever you are.

4. Click the arrow button in the upper-left corner to return to the previous screen.

5. Click the controls in the lower-right corner just as you would click them in any other media player. These controls work with both audio and video playback.

6. Click the mouse button on the Windows Media Player features in the center of the screen. You can also scroll through them using your keyboard's arrow keys and any remote control that might have been included with your laptop.

7. Click the box icon in the upper-right corner to switch between a standard-size window and full-screen view. Full-screen view obscures everything on the screen, including the taskbar.

8. Click the X in the upper-right corner to close Windows Media Player.

 Windows Media Center functions with a variety of different equipment and controls, depending on the manufacturer of your laptop. Check those instructions to see what hardware is available to you.

Figure 23-1: Basic Windows Media Player controls

Change the Way You View Windows Media Center

1. With Windows Media Center open, navigate to Tasks and click Settings.

2. Click the General button to see the menu choices shown in Figure 23-2.

3. Click the Startup and Window Behavior link and select the Windows Media Center Window Always On Top check box to keep the player in view at all times. Click Save.

4. Click the Back arrow in the upper-left corner and click the Visual and Sound Effects link (see Figure 23-3).

5. Click the radio button to select a color scheme for the Windows Media Center screens.

6. Use the plus or minus buttons in the Video Background Color section to specify how empty space is displayed while playing videos. Click Save when you're done.

7. Move your mouse and click the green Start button in the upper-left corner to return to the main screen.

 Windows Media Player tends to take over a system while running, and the tips in this section help give you a little control over how it's displayed on your laptop.

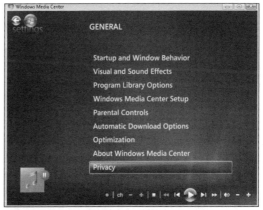

Figure 23-2: General settings in Windows Media Player

Figure 23-3: Choosing Windows Media Player's appearance

Listen to Your Music Library in Windows Media Center

1. In Windows Media Center, navigate to the Music tab.

2. Select Music Library to see a library similar to the one shown in Figure 23-4.

3. Click an album cover to start playing it, or scroll through the views to see headings, such as Artists or Genres.

4. Use the controls shown in Figure 23-5 to control playback. You can also choose to burn tracks to a CD, add tracks to a playlist queue, or edit a track's information.

5. Click the Back arrow in the upper-left corner twice to return to the main music screen. You can continue to use the controls to specify playback options.

6. Click the More Music link to play music from several different network sources.

7. Click Play All to put all your music tracks in the queue.

8. If your laptop has broadcast-radio hardware, you can click Radio to start playback from your chosen station.

9. Click Search to find music on your laptop.

 Windows Media Center looks for music from all sources, including optical discs and any external hard drives connected to your system. You can control the Media Center from this screen.

Figure 23-4: The music library

Figure 23-5: Playing back music

View Pictures and Videos in Windows Media Center

1. In Windows Media Center, scroll to Pictures + Videos, shown in Figure 23-6.

2. Click the Picture Library link to see all pictures in your My Pictures folder. Click Slide Show to view them in a presentation.

3. Click the Back arrow and click the More Pictures link to see other photos from online sources.

4. Click the Play All link to see all your photos in a slide show.

5. Click Video Library to view the files in your My Videos folder.

6. Click the green Start button in the upper-left corner to return to the main menu.

7. Navigate to TV + Movies and click Play DVD, shown in Figure 23-7.

8. With a DVD in the optical drive, use the controls to watch the DVD inside Windows Media Center. You can also use the mouse to control playback.

9. Click the More TV and Internet TV options to view online television from this section.

 Windows Media Center has access to many online features that you may not be able to see in other places. Be sure to check them out when you have the chance.

Figure 23-6: Pictures and videos

Figure 23-7: The Windows Media Center DVD player

Check Out Online Media in Windows Media Center

1. In Windows Media Center, navigate to Online Media, shown in Figure 23-8.

2. Click the Explore link to see the options shown in Figure 23-9.

3. The Showcase option shows all options available from the Online Media area.

4. Scroll through the types of media at the top to focus on what you're interested in.

5. To start playback, click a selection that interests you.

6. Click the Back arrow to see other available options in the Online Media area.

 The Online Media area changes often, depending on which selections Microsoft chooses to feature. Check back often.

 Some of these online media options require you to download software or pay a usage fee. Be aware of what you're getting into when you start clicking.

Figure 23-8: The Online Media link

Figure 23-9: Online media showcase

Link Windows Media Center with Other Devices

1. In Windows Media Center, navigate to Tasks, shown in Figure 23-10.

2. Attach your portable media player to your computer and click the Sync link to move files from Windows Media Center and your library to your player.

3. Click the Add Extender link to connect Windows Media Center to an external connector that transmits media to another device, such as a video game system or a television.

4. Navigate to TV + Movies, shown in Figure 23-11.

5. Click the Set Up TV link to connect your laptop to any broadcast-TV device that might have been included with your laptop.

 Being able to follow these steps depends on any additional hardware you may have. Windows Media Center has the capability to extend to several different devices, but the specific details depend on what you purchase — and you have many choices.

Figure 23-10: Attaching an external device to Windows Media Center

Figure 23-11: Setting up Windows Media Center for television

Index

• *P* •

• Y •

• Z •